# THE KEYS TO THE
# CHRONICLES

# THE KEYS TO THE
# CHRONICLES

## Unlocking the Symbols of
## C. S. Lewis's Narnia

# Marvin D. Hinten

BROADMAN
& HOLMAN
PUBLISHERS

NASHVILLE, TENNESSEE

Ten-Digit ISBN: 0–8054–4028–3
Thirteen-Digit ISBN: 978–0–8054–4028–7

Published by Broadman & Holman Publishers
Nashville, Tennessee

Dewey Decimal Classification: 813
Subject Heading: LEWIS C. S. CHRONICLES OF NARNIA
CHARACTERISTICS IN LITERATURE
RELIGION IN LITERATURE

2 3 4 5 6 7 8 9 10   10 09 08 07 06

# Contents

# Acknowledgments

Portions of this book previously appeared in *The Lamp-Post,* a C. S. Lewis journal for which I am a contributing editor. Thanks to editor David Clark for permission to use that material here.

Professionally, this book is dedicated to Bruce Edwards of Bowling Green State University and Leonard Goss of Broadman & Holman Publishers. This book originated with a doctoral dissertation. Bruce, as my dissertation director, penciled in helpful notes on virtually every page. His Lewis Web site at http://personal.bgsu.edu/~edwards/lewis.html is packed full of information about Lewis. Len Goss's enthusiasm for C. S. Lewis and this book helped ensure its publication. I share his expressed desire that this book will "minister to a great many readers."

Personally, this book is dedicated to my mother, Lorraine Hinten, and my wife, Nancy. Mom instilled in me a love for books at an early age. I still fondly recall our evenings doing dishes together during the 1960s when every night, while Mom washed and I dried, she patiently permitted me to read aloud to her my favorite books, such as *Cheaper by the Dozen* and *The Incredible Journey.* (I would put a saltshaker on the left-hand page and a pepper shaker on the right-hand page to keep my hands free for using the towel.) Thanks, Mom. Nancy loves and supports me in too many ways to list on a single page, but in the literary realm (besides being my crossword puzzle partner), she constantly reads and thinks so we can have quality conversation together. She always says positive things about me, so naturally I consider her a woman of profound judgment. Thanks, Sweetie!

# An Introduction: "Further Up and Further In"

Where does the name *Aslan* come from? What are some of the key Bible references in The Chronicles of Narnia? When Digory Kirk is considering whether to steal an apple in *The Magician's Nephew*, why is there a huge bird in the apple tree watching him? How do Lewis's feelings about prunes show up in *Prince Caspian*? Did Lewis make up names like *Puddleglum* and *Emeth*?

Most adult readers of C. S. Lewis's Narnian Chronicles wonder about these and many other questions. They can tell that certain story elements have a second layer of meaning below the surface. Aslan's death and resurrection, for instance, is clearly analogous to the death and resurrection of Christ in our world. But what else lies below the surface?

That is the purpose of this book—to show you the wonderful assortment of borrowings, allusions, and parallels Lewis blended together to make the magnificent Chronicles of Narnia. Like you, I love this series, both for the stories and for their insights into spiritual life. Perhaps unlike you, I have had an occupation (English professor) that has allowed and encouraged me to study them in more depth, especially to see what went into their making. My doctoral specialization was British Renaissance literature, Lewis's field, and my dissertation was entitled *Parallels and Allusions in C. S. Lewis's Narnian Chronicles,* so I have given years of my life to reading what Lewis read and considering what he did with it. I have admired and enjoyed Lewis's inventiveness in polishing up the treasures of his reading, and I hope you do too!

    —Dr. Marv Hinten, English Dept., Friends University, Wichita KS (hintenm@friends.edu)

    (Feel free to e-mail me if you have questions or comments.)

# CHAPTER 1

# Lewis, the Chronicles, Allusions, and Allegory

During the year 2000 *Christianity Today* planned an issue on the one hundred major Christian books written in English during the twentieth century. But the issue never took place as planned. The problem: As their survey results began to come in, the editors noticed that almost all the books near the top of the list were by C. S. Lewis. In fact, had they stuck by their original plan of covering the one hundred most important Christian books of the past century, the list would have looked like C. S. Lewis and the Seven Dwarfs! So they wisely allotted Lewis the top position and moved on from there. (If you would like a refresher course on the life and writings of Lewis, turn to Appendix A for a brief overview.)

*Mere Christianity* may be Lewis's most important religious work, at least according to surveys, but his children's fantasy series, The Chronicles of Narnia, (hereafter Chronicles), are surely his best loved. Lewis began writing the books in the late 1940s. They were published annually from 1950 to 1956 as follows, with the abbreviated names used in this book in parentheses:

*The Lion, the Witch and the Wardrobe (Lion)* (1950)
*Prince Caspian (Caspian)* (1951)
*The Voyage of the "Dawn Treader" (Treader)* (1952)
*The Silver Chair (Chair)* (1953)

*The Horse and His Boy* (*Horse*) (1954)
*The Magician's Nephew* (*Nephew*) (1955)
*The Last Battle* (*Battle*) (1956)

Although for four decades the books were numbered in publication order, in 1994 HarperCollins, taking over the standard paperback edition from Macmillan, numbered the series in chronological order. Arguments can be made for reading the series either way; this book uses the traditional numbering.

Lewis began writing *Lion* about 1948 after an abortive attempt nearly a decade earlier. Some writers have suggested that a difficult philosophical debate at the Socratic Club with Oxford philosopher Elizabeth Anscombe may have moved him away from apologetics and toward fantasy. According to his friend George Sayer, after the debate Lewis said to him about apologetic works, "I can never write another book of that sort" (308—source references are at the end of the book in the "Works Cited" section). Biographer A. N. Wilson claims *Lion* "grew out of Lewis's . . . defeat at the hands of Elizabeth Anscombe at the Socratic Club" (220). Or it may be that, having written *The Problem of Pain, Mere Christianity,* and *Miracles* within the past decade, Lewis simply felt he had carried philosophical apologetics as far as he needed to, or possibly even as far as was good for him. In an August 2, 1946, letter to Dorothy Sayers, he remarked that apologetic writing was "dangerous to one's own faith" (*Letters* 382). Whatever the reason for returning, when Lewis began the Narnia books in earnest, he finished the entire series within six years.

As of 1993 Colin Manlove estimated that well over twenty million people had read the Chronicles (20). With the surging interest since then in children's fantasy (*Harry Potter*) and the Tolkien /Lewis circle (*Lord of the Rings*), the past several years have undoubtedly increased that number by millions more. Certainly a key reason for the popularity of the series is its spiritual content; many Christian parents buy the Chronicles for their children and read the books aloud to them as quality family time. Numerous American schoolteachers, particularly in the first few elementary years, read the books aloud to their students for the same reasons that Laura Ingalls Wilder's *Little House* series is frequently read: the books involve children as characters, involve a noncontemporary setting, are morally wholesome, and are part of a series, which solves the "what to read next" problem. With the increasing attention in many school districts to character education, or "teaching the virtues," the Chronicles are likely to remain a staple of classroom reading for many years to come.

Like most great children's books, such as *Alice in Wonderland* and *Huckleberry Finn,* the Chronicles operate on two levels, with a secondary, sophisticated layer available only to adults—and even then only to adults with a certain level of background knowledge. The books are permeated with subtle references to literature, Christianity, linguistics, mythology, and other areas. These references, whether in Lewis or other writers, are given various names in the study of literature: allusions, parallels, analogues, allegorical elements, etc. Lewis scholars disagree about how allegorical the Chronicles are and whether it's important to try to determine the sources Lewis used and what he did with them. For a fuller study of these issues, see Appendix B.

Whether one finds tracing allusions to be a useful tool in understanding the Chronicles, one thing remains clear to almost any adult reader: C. S. Lewis was a remarkably allusive writer, especially in The Chronicles of Narnia, where he borrows from other sources in virtually every chapter. What makes his books so allusive? Why was this such a natural format for Lewis? Two key reasons are these: Lewis read and remembered far more than other writers, and he believed and followed the medieval/Renaissance tradition of telling the old stories rather than producing something entirely new.

To say Lewis read and remembered more than other writers is understatement. In the memoir collection *In Search of C. S. Lewis,* contributors repeatedly provide stunning examples of Lewis's prodigious memory. One of the most astounding comes from a Lewis student of the 1950s (later a *London Observer* drama critic), Kenneth Tynan, who said Lewis had "the most astonishing memory of any man I have ever known" (Schofield 6). As evidence, Tynan cited a "game" he and Lewis played in which Tynan would pick a book, page, and line from Lewis's shelves at random, and Lewis would "always" identify the book and "was usually able to quote the rest of the page" (Schofield 7).

It is hard not to greet an episode like this with skepticism. But Lewis lore is filled with similar incidents. Stephen Schofield recalls a similar incident from the 1950s, a conversation between Rhodes scholar Richard Selig and Lewis in which Lewis claimed to

"remember everything I've ever read and bits pop up uninvited."

"Surely not everything you've ever read, Mr. Lewis?"

"Yes everything, Selig, even the most boring texts."

Unable to let this pass, Selig went to the college library, found an obscure poem, brought it back to the group, and read a bit. Lewis then recited the next ten lines. As Schofield puts it, "Conversation was slow to resume at that end of the table." (164)

One cannot help wondering whether years and reputation have inflated the accounts. (When your grandparents tell how hard their lives were, how they had to walk miles and miles to school in bad weather, doesn't it seem like it used to rain four days a week back then, with uphill roads both ways?) Inflated or not, however, the stories clearly indicate a man with astonishing powers of recall—even, according to E. L. Edmonds, for student essays written years earlier (Schofield 41). Lewis sometimes forgot details of his own novels, but the writings of others became a part of him.

And these writings were not few. The extent of Lewis's reading was prodigious and, to those hardy souls who have attempted to follow in his footsteps, awe-inspiring. Numerous scholars have been tempted, in a laudable effort to understand Lewis better, to read as much as possible of what he read. One begins with a good will, soon feels daunted, then overwhelmed, and finally defeated. To understand the herculean nature of such a task, let us imagine an attempt simply to gain familiarity with all of Lewis's literary allusions on the first ten pages of one typical piece of nonfiction: his essay "On Science Fiction" (*On Stories* 59). These few pages contain references to all of the following literary works:

| | |
|---|---|
| *The Time Machine* | *The First Men in the Moon* |
| *Tom's A-Cold* | *Brave New World* |
| *1984* | *The Waves* |
| *20,000 Leagues under the Sea* | *The Land Ironclads* |
| *Prelude to Space* | "The Battle of Maldon" |
| *Arcadia* | "Lepanto" |
| *Inferno* | Iter Extaticum Celeste |
| *Gulliver's Travels* | *Alice in Wonderland* |
| *Everyman* | *The Ancient Mariner* |
| "Essay on Man" | *The Odyssey* |
| *Last and First Men* | *When the Sleeper Awakes* |
| *The End of the World* | Possible Worlds |
| *Childhood's End* | *Many Dimensions* |
| Marchen | *Beowulf* |
| She | *King Solomon's Mines* |
| The Brass Bottle | *Flatland* |

All these works are specifically referred to in just ten pages! It's an impressive list. The last one-third of the essay refers to another twenty-four works, and this list does not include authors mentioned without specific works. Altogether, approximately sixty authors and works are commented upon in this one medium-length essay (not written for publication, I should add, but merely presented as a talk to an English club and published after Lewis's death).

The list makes clear the breadth not only of Lewis's reading but of his retention as well, which is perhaps even more impressive. Like a full bucket under a streaming tap, Lewis was continually replenished with images and phrases that spilled over into his own writing. When we further recognize that Lewis used not only literary references in his writing, but theological, linguistic, biographical, autographical, mythological, historical, and biblical ones as well, it is clear that for anyone studying Lewis's use of allusions, the cup runs over.

Lewis's other notable characteristic as a joint critic/theologian /novelist was his appreciation of tradition. It could almost be called veneration, although Lewis did write and enjoy science fiction, a relatively modern genre. But at any given point in his career, if asked whether he preferred the present way of doing things or the way it had been done forty years ago, he would probably have preferred the past, whether the choices involved transportation (he didn't drive), communication (he didn't type), or poetry (he didn't write free verse).

This attitude carried over into his novels, where more often than not Lewis followed the method generally favored by authors until the start of this century: to tell stories that had already been told. To many contemporary readers, this desire to build on someone else's foundation seems less praiseworthy than erecting a building from scratch. But to most medieval and Renaissance writers, originality was less important than the quality of the final product. Surely the odds were better of finding a good story among the old "auctores" (authors) than of being able to create one independently. Isaac Newton's comment about being able to see farther because he stood on the shoulders of giants was seen as true not only of science, where the building process was evident, but of literature as well.

C. S. Lewis was perhaps more a product of medieval and Renaissance thinking than any other twentieth-century writer. Significantly, he was named to the chair of medieval and Renaissance poetry at Cambridge during the publication of the Chronicles, showing how his literary and fictional interests flourished simultaneously. Like the medieval and Renaissance writers on whom he lectured, Lewis respected traditional associations. A noteworthy early example from the Chronicles appears in the sixth chapter of *Lion,* where the children are being led to an unknown destination by a robin. Edmund suggests the robin may be an evildoer, luring them into a trap. Peter reflects on the possibility, then decides against it by remarking significantly, "Still—a robin you know. They're good birds in all the stories I've ever read. I'm sure a robin wouldn't be on the wrong side" (59).

Lewis's allegiance to established symbolism comes from his view that most symbols become established because they resonate certain values. In his "personal heresy" controversy with E. M. W. Tillyard, Lewis observes: "A poetic symbol—like the rose, for Love, in Guillaume de Lorris—comes trailing clouds of glory from the real world, clouds whose shape and colour largely determine and explain its poetic use. In an equation, x and y will do as well as a and b; but the *Romance of the Rose* could not, without loss, be re-written as the *Romance of the Onion,* and if a man did not see why, we could only send him back to the real world to study roses, onions, and love" (*Heresy* 97).

And like a good medieval author, Lewis used the "kitchen sink" approach to his materials. In an article on "Imagination and Thought in the Middle Ages," Lewis offers a penetrating insight into the medieval scholar's mind: "It was apparently difficult to believe that anything in the books—so costly, fetched from so far, so old, often so lovely to the eye and hand, was just plumb wrong. No; if Seneca and St. Paul disagreed with one another, and both with Cicero, and all these with Boethius, there must be some explanation which would harmonize them" (*Studies* 45).

C. S. Lewis read everything, remembered everything, and used everything. That statement may be hyperbolic, but it's probably less hyperbolic for Lewis than for any other twentieth-century author. Thus his works are filled with allusions, parallels, and analogues. While source studies are of value with any author, this is particularly true of Lewis, who borrowed from so many different places, in a manner that has sometimes led to confusion and sometimes (as in the case of Tolkien) to irritation. Some people enjoy the multiple layers, some do not, but in either case we appreciate Lewis's writing skill more if we can first try to determine as fully as possible what he was doing.

Finally, before we begin, I want to invite you to be amazed. I think Christians need to cultivate the ability to be filled with wonder—at linden trees, at cataract surgery, at Beethoven piano sonatas, even at diet cola! And so I encourage you, during the next seven chapters, to enjoy seeing what inventiveness focused on glorifying God can do. Book by book we will proceed through the pages, looking at the wonderful variety of images Lewis worked into his writing.

# CHAPTER 2

# "Deeper Magic": Allusions in *The Lion, the Witch and the Wardrobe*

*The Lion, the Witch and the Wardrobe* is the most clearly biblical of the seven Chronicles, incorporating numerous elements of the suffering, death, and resurrection of Christ. It was not Lewis's original intent to rewrite the life of Christ as a children's fairy tale. As he noted in an article on fairy tales:

> Some people seem to think that I began by asking myself how I could say something about Christianity to children; then fixed on the fairy tale as an instrument; then collected information about child psychology and decided what age-group I'd write for; then drew up a list of basic Christian truths and hammered out "allegories" to embody them. This is all pure moonshine. I couldn't write in that way at all. Everything began with images; a faun carrying an umbrella, a queen on a sledge, a magnificent lion. At first there wasn't even anything Christian about them; that element pushed itself in of its own accord (*On Stories* 46).

When Lewis first tried to form these images into a story in 1939, there indeed doesn't appear to be anything biblical about them: "This book is about four children whose names were Ann, Martin, Rose, and Peter. But it is most about Peter who was the youngest"

(Hooper 29–30). This contains two significant differences from the actual opening, which Lewis wrote in the late 1940s: "Once there were four children whose names were Peter, Susan, Edmund and Lucy" (1). In the original attempt Ann would have presumably been the oldest, which generally carries some leadership responsibilities; the alteration puts Peter in the headship role, which Lewis always felt belonged to a male. In addition, since the children to a considerable degree play the role of Aslan's disciples in the book, the name change identifies Peter (later the "High King") with Peter, the traditional head of the apostles in our world.

Jesus had three disciples, Peter, James, and John, who formed a sort of inner circle, being present at situations such as the transfiguration and the garden of Gethsemane prayer that the other apostles missed. It is not too fanciful to see Peter, Susan, and Lucy as analogues to these three. (Since Lewis did not originally plan a sequel, he did not realize at this time that Susan would later leave the "disciples.") If Peter parallels the apostle Peter, then Lucy parallels John, the disciple "whom Jesus loved," as he is repeatedly described in the book of John (20:2, 21:7, etc.). Throughout the series Lucy is the one most dedicated to goodness and the one to whom Aslan appears most frequently and displays the most tenderness. Her name likely was suggested by the name of Owen Barfield's daughter, to whom Lewis as "affectionate Godfather" dedicated the book. Owen Barfield was Lewis's lifelong attorney and friend.

The idea to have the four children leave London and stay with a single professor during the war was based on reality. Lewis and his household kept several children from London "because of the air-raids," as the novel says. The adventures start because a "steady rain falling" forces the children to explore the house, "the sort of house that you never seem to come to the end of" (4). In his autobiography Lewis says, "I am a product of long corridors [and] . . . attics explored in solitude," which he examined during "endless rainy afternoons" (Joy 10).

Upon entering the land of Narnia, which Lewis secretary Walter Hooper notes is named after an "ancient Italian city" (108), Lucy meets the faun Mr. Tumnus, whose name seems an abbreviated form of Vertumnus, the Roman god of the seasons and of growth. And I think we are indeed meant to be reminded of the mythological name, for it was through the power of Vertumnus that the seasons changed and growth took place. Yet in Narnia, the faun Tumnus obviously has no power, and Narnia is a land (at least when we meet Tumnus) where the seasons never change and nothing ever grows. The name would have been familiar to Lewis from a variety of sources; besides its appearance in Greek myth in general, Ovid tells the story of Vertumnus in the *Metamorphoses,* and Milton mentions him in *Paradise Lost* (9.395). (The goddess that Vertumnus chases in Ovid, Pomona, is mentioned in *Prince Caspian.*)

Vertumnus asks Lucy whether she is a "Daughter of Eve." This roundabout way of referring to humans may have been suggested by *Paradise Lost* (4.324–25), which speaks of "Adam the goodliest man of men since born / His Sons, the fairest of her Daughters Eve" (286). "Sons of Adam" effectively distinguishes the humans from the animals, since *adam* is Hebrew for man.

Literary scholar C. W. Manlove has suggested that Tumnus's relationship with Lucy parallels the White Rabbit's relationship with Alice in Wonderland. I find that unconvincing and should perhaps here note that this book by no means attempts to cover all the allusions and parallels that have been suggested for the Chronicles but only the ones I have uncovered myself or have found most significant and/or convincing in other criticism. Since Lewis uses so many allusions, which is similar to his abundant use of analogies in his nonfiction, people occasionally become hooked on finding symbolism everywhere. This book limits itself to the parallels and allusions that seem most likely.

When Lucy tells Tumnus she has entered Narnia through the wardrobe in the spare room, he refers to her as the girl from "the far land of Spare Oom where eternal summer reigns around the bright city of War Drobe" (11). Brian Sibley suggests a source for this in Edith Nesbitt's *The Aunt and Anabel,* where the magic land is reached via "Bigwardrobeinspareroom" (*Land of Narnia* 21).

When Peter and Susan hear Lucy's unbelievable tale of Narnia, they take their concern to the professor with whom they are staying. Though his name is not revealed in *Lion* (presumably Lewis had not determined it yet), we learn in *Nephew* that this is Digory Kirke, a surname filled with meaning for Lewis. *Kirk* is Old Norse (as well as Scottish) for "church"; thus, at least indirectly, the children find their way to Aslan's country through the church. In fact, Lewis had already used *kirk* for "church" in his 1930s allegory, *The Pilgrim's Regress*. Edmund Spenser's use of the word in his epic poem *The Faerie Queene* may have nudged Lewis toward it as well. And on a different but equally applicable level, *Kirk* is short for Kirkpatrick, the retired professor who served as a tutor during Lewis's teenage years and for whom he always retained the utmost respect. With one word Lewis is thus able to invest the story with literary, linguistic, and biographical layers.

During Peter and Susan's conversations with Professor Kirke occurs the first example of what I call "autography"—Lewis's borrowing of phrases or concepts from his adult theological nonfiction for his children's fiction. Professor Kirke asks the children to think about Lucy and her improbable story logically: "There are only three possibilities. Either your sister is telling lies, or she is mad, or she is telling the truth. You know she doesn't tell lies and it is obvious that she is not mad. For the moment then and unless any further evidence turns up, we must assume that she is telling the truth" (45).

It would be difficult for anyone familiar with *Mere Christianity* to read this and not be reminded of Lewis's famous "liar, lunatic, or Lord" trichotomy. Here is the relevant passage from that book: "A man who was merely a man and said the sort of things Jesus said would not be a great moral teacher. He would either be a lunatic—on a level with the man who says he is a poached egg—or else he would be the Devil of Hell. You must make your choice. Either this man was, and is, the Son of God: or else a madman or something worse" (*Mere* 56).

Lewis claimed not to have begun with theology in mind; but certainly theology was in his mind (at least in revision) by this early point, approximately one-fourth of the way into the novel.

When the four children finally enter Narnia together, they see a sign proclaiming the wrath of Queen Jadis, the White Witch, signed by her wolf police captain, known in the earlier American editions as Fenris Ulf. (In British editions, and the revised American edition, he is "Maugrim," with obvious connotations of "grim maw," meaning "fierce mouth"). The queen's name "Jadis" is a French word meaning "of old," as in Francois Villon's medieval lyric, "Ballade des Dames de Temps Jadis," or "Ballad of the Women of Yesteryear." The word certainly fits a being who has been alive for well over a thousand years. In addition, *Jadis* has the connotations of "false jade," which is used elsewhere in the Chronicles by Lewis (*Horse* 105) as a term of abuse. (In the Renaissance and into the twentieth century, a jade was a broken-down horse, also called a nag; by a play on the word *nag*, jade came to mean a "shrewish woman.") The witch has made it always winter in Narnia, corresponding to the dreaded perpetual winter, or *fimbulvetr*, of Norse myth (Davidson 202). For ancient Scandinavian people, living so near the Arctic, the worst plight imaginable would be to live in a land where spring thaw never came. So that fear was woven into their mythology, and Lewis pictures the myth here.

As for the witch's captain, "ulf" is Old Norse for wolf, and Fenris is clearly a form of Fenrir (the wolf-son of the evil god Loki in Norse mythology), who bit off the hand of Tyr, god of victory. Fenrir is traditionally a symbol of fierceness and destruction; at Ragnarok, the ending of the world in Norse myth, it is he who destroys Odin, chief of all the Norse gods. Fenris's close association with the witch parallels Fenrir's close association with Loki, the evil Norse god.

The children hear from Mr. Beaver about Aslan, the Christ figure of the Chronicles. Aslan is, fittingly, a lion because the lion is traditionally labeled the "king of beasts" (as Mr. Beaver proclaims Aslan, with a capital K, in the eighth chapter). In addition, "Lion of the tribe of Judah" is one of the biblical names for Christ, as in Revelation 5:5, where under that name Christ demonstrates his power by opening seven previously unbroken seals. *Aslan,* the Turkish word for "lion," Lewis gleaned from Edward Lane's translation of *Arabian Nights,* according to a 1952 letter (*Letters to Children* 29).

Why was Lewis reading translations of *Arabian Nights* shortly before writing *Lion*? In the late 1940s he had a Middle Eastern pupil, M. A. Manzalaoui, who eventually did his Oxford thesis on the subject of pre-twentieth-century English translations of Arabic works. Edward Lane was a nineteenth-century English writer who did one of the main Victorian-era translations of *Arabian Nights.* Given Lewis's conscientious efforts as a thesis director, I imagine he reread Lane's translation while working with Manazlaoui as a student, and thus the word *Aslan* had been on his mind a good bit as he prepared to begin the Chronicles.

The Turkish derivation of the word *Aslan* appears to be, by the way, perhaps the only exception in the Chronicles to the rule that anything Arabic or Turkish-sounding or favoring Turkish ways is bad. (Remember that the witch had won Edmund to her side with Turkish delight.) For medieval Christians (and thus for Lewis) the Arabs were the feared villains from the South who nearly conquered Europe in the eighth century, and the Turks were the infidels who had taken the holy city of Jerusalem and spilled so much Christian blood during the Crusades.

After Mr. Beaver quotes one of the "old rhymes" (the Narnian equivalent of prophecy), he tells the children about the witch, who is descended on one side from giants and on the other side from the Jinn. In Norse mythology the giants perpetually undermined the work of the gods. The Jinn were supernatural creatures of Arabic legend with the power to take on human and animal shapes. (Yes, this is the same creature as a genie, appearing from a rubbed-up lamp; one occasionally sees the word spelled *jinni,* showing its heritage.) Lewis grew up with Norse mythology, and as just noted, he spent much of the late 1940s rereading Arabian myth.

Mr. Beaver tells the children four thrones are waiting for human rulers at Cair Paravel, the seacoast city which should serve as

Narnia's capital. The city's name may stem from a rhythmic extension of *caravel*. Caravels were the sailing vessels that began to be used in Europe in the fifteenth century; two of Columbus's three ships, including his flagship, were caravels (Chamberlin 29). In addition, *cair* is an Old Norse word, taken into Middle English, meaning "to go." It was used occasionally to form Norse place-names; thus J. R. R. Tolkien uses it as part of the name of Cair Andros, an island in *The Return of the King* (103).

The Beavers and the children flee from the witch across the countryside and meet Father Christmas. This figure particularly drew Tolkien's ire as an intrusion of legend into a section of the story related to the coming of Christ into the world. It's interesting to note in Brian Sibley's *The Land of Narnia* a picture of Lewis as a child beside what Sibley labels one of his favorite toys—Father Christmas riding on a donkey. That toy would seem in itself a blending of two elements of Christmas, for the donkey, in combination with the season, suggests the one Mary rode on her trip from Galilee to Bethlehem. Even as a preschooler Lewis seems to have had an instinctive pleasure in mixing religious and mythical elements together.

Father Christmas distributes gifts to the children, which, in another blending, somewhat parallel the spiritual gifts given to the church. Peter is given a shield and a sword. In the familiar "whole armor of God" passage in Ephesians 6, the shield is faith and the sword is the Word of God. Susan receives a horn which can bring help, analogous to prayer, and Lucy receives a cordial with supernatural restorative powers, representing the gift of healing. (Susan also receives a bow and arrows; if this has a spiritual parallel, I am unable to determine it. But with Lewis, unlike Tolkien and most other writers, the most common technique is to blend allusive and nonallusive elements.)

As Father Christmas is to some extent allied with Aslan, the gifts also have a Norse flavor. The most common poetic name for *king* in Anglo-Saxon and Old Norse poetry is "ring-giver" (sometimes "gift-giver"). Aslan, the lord of Narnia, is distributing gifts to his followers through Father Christmas, similar to what occurred in Norse myth: "Like any earthly ruler, Odin [the chief Norse god] handed out weapons to his chosen followers, and once they had received them, they were bound to give him loyal service till death and beyond it" (Davidson 49). This moving back and forth from the spiritual (Aslan) to the secular (Father Christmas) to the secular with spiritual overtones (the gifts), with Norse elements thrown in, is characteristically Lewisian.

The children and the Beavers arrive at the Stone Table, which is located, significantly, on a hilltop, since this is to be the place of Aslan's sacrifice, and Christian tradition has for centuries placed Calvary (where Christ was crucified) on a hill. Lewis himself asserted, in a 1960 letter, that the Stone Table represented (he said "is") Moses' table (*Letters to Children* 93). This "table" is another word for the stone tablets upon which the Ten Commandments were inscribed, as described in Exodus 32:16: "And the tables were the work of God, and the writing was the writing of God, graven upon the tables." (All biblical references are to the King James Version, called the Authorised Version in England, since that was the version Lewis knew and used throughout his life; when that wording is unclear, I provide modern language in brackets.) This parallel to the Ten Commandments explains both the age and the carved writing on the Stone Table and provides an additional reason for the hilltop location, since the Ten Commandments were given on the top of Mount Sinai. The pavilion (tent) "hard by" the Stone Table reminds one of the tabernacle, the tent of God's presence for the Old Testament Jews.

Aslan's creatures by the Stone Table include an assorted mix of humans, animals, and mythological creatures; among these last are four centaurs and "a bull with the head of a man" (122). A few pages later we read of other creatures who are also a mix of animal and human, but they fight on the witch's side. When creatures appear whose bodies are a mix of half animal, half human, how does Lewis decide whether they will serve good or evil? Throughout the Chronicles, creatures with a human head and animal body are good;

creatures with a human body and animal head are bad. This symbolically represents the standard Renaissance concept of reason over passion, emphasized so repeatedly by Milton in *Paradise Lost*—that in the great chain of being, reason should always be elevated over passion and control it. Some of the witch's creatures, noted on page 132, are minotaurs, with human bodies and bull heads, symbolizing their perverse commitment to passion over reason; thus they join the side of evil.

When Aslan's troops rescue Edmund, they are unable to attack the witch effectively because she has taken on the appearance of a boulder: "It was part of her magic that she could make things look like what they weren't" (135). One of her affinities with Loki of Norse mythology has already been mentioned (the wolf sidekick); this is another, for Loki also had the ability to change his shape, in various episodes becoming flea, bird, horse, fly, salmon, and woman. The Jinn of Arabian mythology had this power as well, and as Mr. Beaver notes, the witch is descended from the Jinn.

Another element of Norse mythology appears with Aslan addressing the witch's dwarf as "Son of Earth" (136). Dwarfs were literally thought in Norse myth to have been generated by the earth. As High One explains to Gangleri in Snorri Sturluson's thirteenth-century version of it: "Then the gods seated themselves on their thrones and held counsel, and remembered how dwarfs had quickened in the earth and under the soil like maggots in flesh. The dwarfs had first emerged and come to life in Ymir's flesh, and at that time were maggots. But by the decree of the gods they acquired human understanding and the appearance of men, although they lived in the earth and in rocks" (41).

When the witch confronts Aslan, she reminds him of the "Deep Magic," that "every traitor belongs to me as my lawful prey and that for every treachery I have a right to a kill" (139). This seems an oblique reference to Romans 6:23a, "The wages of sin is death." The word *lawful* is appropriately chosen, as the magic is written on the Stone Table, which represents the requirements of the Old Testament law. It is also written (in the American editions before

1994) on "the World Ash Tree," another blending of Norse with Christian elements. While the Stone Table (which according to the White Witch has been used for sacrifice before) is a symbol of death, the World Ash Tree, or Yggdrasill, was a Norse symbol of life. Dew from this tree provided nourishment for two humans while the rest of the world was undergoing the long winter (Davidson 202). Symbolically, then, the Old Testament provided nourishment during the time before the sacrifice of Christ.

The witch tells Aslan that because of Edmund's treachery the law of Narnia requires that she be given blood, a fairly clear reference to (among other passages) Hebrews 9:22: "And almost all things are by the law purged with blood; and without shedding of blood there is no remission [forgiveness]." If this is not accomplished, Narnia will be destroyed with fire and water, which immediately reminds biblically literate readers of Noah's flood and the prophesied final destruction of the Earth by fire.

Edmund feels during this scene as though he ought to say or do something, but "a moment later he felt that he was not expected to do anything except to wait" (140). Perhaps this is a bit fanciful, but Lewis loved John Milton, writing one entire book just on his writing; and that last word, combined with the idea presented, bears some similarity to the closing line of Milton's sonnet on his blindness: "They also serve who only stand and wait."

The fourteenth chapter of *Lion,* "Aslan's Passion," is the most biblically allusive chapter of the Chronicles. The similarities in this portion primarily need recognition rather than comment, so I will simply list them here, first the *Lion* section, then the parallel biblical passage.

At last Peter said, "But you will be there yourself, Aslan." "I can give you no promise of that," answered the *Lion.* (143)

Simon Peter said unto him, Lord, whither goest thou? Jesus answered him, Whither I go, thou canst not follow me now. (John 13:36a)

18

(Aslan speaking) "I am sad and lonely. Lay your hands on my mane so that I can feel you are there and let us walk like that." (147)

Then saith he [Jesus] unto them, My soul is exceeding sorrowful, even unto death: tarry ye here, and watch with me. (Matt. 26:38)

Had the Lion chosen, one of those paws could have been the death of them all. (149)

"Thinkest thou that I cannot now pray to my Father, and he shall presently give me more than twelve legions of angels?" (Matt. 26:53)

But he made no noise. (150)

But Jesus held his peace. (Matt. 26:63)

Thickly was he surrounded by the whole crowd of creatures kicking him, hitting him, spitting on him, jeering at him. (151)

Then did they spit in his face, and buffeted him. (Matt. 26:67a) And the men that held Jesus mocked him, and smote [hit] him. (Luke 22:63)

At the end of the chapter, Aslan dies. In the middle of the night, Susan and Lucy try to untie him but are unable to. This parallels Mark 16:3, when the women on their way to the tomb recognize that they'll be unable to move the stone. (In the novel and in the Bible, both groups caring about the body are entirely female.) But mice come along that are able to gnaw away the ropes, thus solving the plot problem and bringing in Aesop's fable at the same time. The girls notice that as dawn nears, the stars are "getting fainter—all except one very big one low down on the Eastern horizon" (156–57). In our world this would be Venus, or the morning star, and its presence as Aslan nears resurrection alludes to Christ's referral to himself in Revelation 22:16 as "the bright and morning star."

Aslan's resurrection occurs just as "up came the edge of the sun" (158). Thus the Son (of the Emperor over the Sea) rises as the sun rises. The pun on *sun* and *Son* is a frequent one in seventeenth-century religious poetry. Henry Vaughan calls his poem on attending church "Son-days"; George Herbert, in "The Son," says, "How neatly do we give one only name / To parent's issue and the sun's bright star!" (DiCesare 157, 60).

At Aslan's resurrection the Stone Table cracks, symbolizing the end of the law and perhaps paralleling the tearing in two of the temple veil as well (Matt. 27:51). Just as the apostles in Luke 24:37 "supposed they had seen a spirit," Susan wonders whether Aslan is a ghost. Aslan's response, "Do I look it?" is one of his more informal remarks in the Chronicles. His subsequent rescue of the statues corresponds to the traditional Harrowing of Hell, when (in medieval and Renaissance theology) Jesus rescued the souls of the Jewish patriarchs who had died before him.

Near the end of the book, when the final battle is over, Edmund receives a few drops of the cordial for his wounds and is restored both physically and emotionally/spiritually, possibly in an allusion to James 5:15: "And the prayer of faith shall save the sick, and the Lord shall raise him up; and if he have committed sins, they shall be forgiven him." Lucy notes that Edmund looks the best he has been "since his first term at that horrid school which was where he had begun to go wrong" (177). Although the series is written by an Oxford don (equivalent to a college instructor in this country), schools are not treated favorably in the Chronicles. As any reader of the autobiographical *Surprised by Joy* will recall, Lewis loathed his school days. A man in his fifties who devotes 40 percent of his autobiography to telling how much he hated school has obviously been scarred for life, particularly when he entitles the first chapter on the subject "Concentration Camp." It is well for the series that there are few similar allusions to Lewis's education, for they are not the happiest portions of the Chronicles, in either the literary or the regular sense.

Allusively, *Lion* is the most biblical and most Norse of the Chronicles. This interesting feature reveals a characteristic of Lewis that has been overlooked. While the charges are accurate that he mixes together images from a variety of sources, Lewis generally selects a preponderance of images that will in some way match the setting and/or theme of the book. For a warm, wet climate (as in *Caspian*), Lewis uses a large number of Greek elements; for a warm, dry climate (as in *Horse*), he uses many Arabian/Turkish elements. In the case of *Lion*, much of the Narnian portion of the book is set in the witch's eternal winter. To fit that climate Lewis uses a larger-than-usual number of Norse elements. Lewis does mix together a variety of the elements in each book, but the majority of the elements support the setting. This can also be seen in the next book, *Prince Caspian*.

CHAPTER 3

# "Old Narnia Is True":
# Allusions in *Prince Caspian*

*Caspian* begins with the four Pevensie children returning via a magic call into their former Narnian capital, Cair Paravel. At first, since a long time (in that world) has passed, they do not recognize where they are, though regal aspects of the area cause them to reminisce about their days as kings and queens of Narnia. The "trigger" for Peter finally recognizing where they have landed is the discovery in the grass of "a little chess-knight" (16) made of gold. This scene is modeled after the Norse myth remembrances in the *Prose Edda*. As Snorri Sturluson describes it, the gods (or Aesir) "will all sit down together and converse, calling to mind their hidden lore and talking about things that happened in the past, about . . . the wolf Fenrir. Then they will find there in the grass the golden chessmen the Aesir used to own" (Sturluson 91–92).

Among their recollections the Pevensies remember how a lady named Pomona put a good spell on the fruit orchard. Pomona, in our world, is the Roman goddess of fruit. In Roman myth, she is associated with the plant-growth god Vertumnus, mentioned in the previous chapter.

The Pevensie children suspect ever more strongly that they are in their old capital, but not until they count the number of steps to the treasure chamber does Lucy say, "Then it really must be Cair

22

Paravel" (21). Off hand it does not seem likely for her to know so surely that the way to the chamber involved sixteen steps. How many of us know even the number of stair steps contained in our own homes? But Lewis was a Sherlock Holmes fan (the opening page of *Nephew,* in fact, refers to Holmes by name), and the use of step-counting as an observational tool echoes the first Sherlock Holmes short story ever written, "A Scandal in Bohemia." Holmes and Watson have an exchange about the difference between seeing and observing, and Watson admits that he has used their apartment steps hundreds of times without knowing how many there are. Holmes responds, "I know that there are seventeen steps, because I have both seen and observed" (Doyle 10). (Because of this sentence, I know that there are seventy-three steps to my fourth-floor office; I carefully counted them during my first week of work, just in case anyone should ever need to know. Such is the influence of Sherlock Holmes on fans such as Lewis and me.)

The Pevensies discover that Narnia's rightful king is Caspian, probably named by Lewis after the sea of our world, since he later becomes known as Caspian the Seafarer. Caspian lives with his uncle and aunt, Miraz (a mere ass, perhaps?) and Prunaprismia, a name combining the wrinkled connotations of *prune* and the hyperaffected connotations of *prissy.* (A later character in the book is the despised schoolteacher Miss Prizzle, which can be manufactured from a combination of *prissy* and *drizzle.*) Both *prune* and *prissy* carried pejorative biographical meaning for Lewis. Regarding prissiness, Lewis said in a January 10, 1952, letter that two things he couldn't bear were "a man's man" and "a woman's woman" (*Letters* 417), by which he meant a man who is only interested in sports and mechanical objects and a woman who cares only about "feminine things," a woman such as Susan Pevensie turns out to be. Susan does not make it to Aslan's country in the series, and Jill's scathing remark is that Susan is too interested in "nylons and lipstick and invitations" (*Battle* 135). In short, one of Susan's character flaws is that she was prissy.

As for prunes, Lewis more than once wrote the story of his remarkably strong feelings regarding that food. This is the version in

"On Three Ways of Writing for Children": "Once in a hotel dining-room I said, rather too loudly, 'I loathe prunes.' 'So do I,' came an unexpected six-year-old voice from another table. Sympathy was instantaneous. Neither of us thought it funny. We both knew that prunes are far too nasty to be funny" (*On Stories* 42). The name *Prunaprismia* thus says all we need to know regarding Lewis's feelings about how Caspian's aunt would have raised him.

But, as is usual with Lewis, the name has literary allusiveness as well. In Charles Dickens's lengthy novel *Little Dorrit,* a woman named Mrs. General has made a career of forming the minds and manners of young ladies. She tells her charges that one key attribute for succeeding in polite society, and particularly for succeeding with young gentlemen, is to have well-rounded lips. How does a young lady develop well-rounded lips? According to Mrs. General, the key is to spend time every day saying the words *prunes* and *prism.* The book's main character, Little Dorrit, practices these two words so much that chapter 43 of the novel is entitled "Mostly, Prunes and Prism." So the name *Prunaprismia* derives from a combination of literature and biography, the sort of blending Lewis loved.

Prince Caspian hears the tales of the ancient lands of Narnia from his nurse, who tells him stories each night before he goes to bed. Brian Sibley suggests a biographical connection here with Lewis's own nurse, Lizzie Endicott, who used to tell him as a child exotic tales of long-ago Ireland, stories filled with magic that stirred his imagination (*Land of Narnia* 9).

Caspian's ancestors, he learns, have come from the world of Telmar. Lewis liked to put parts of foreign languages together to form exotic names, a fitting pastime for a man who liked to play Scrabble in multiple languages. In this case, since the inhabitants of Telmar had originally been pirates on the seas of Earth, *Tel* seems short for *Tellus,* Latin for "Earth," joined to *mar,* Latin for "sea." Since Lewis was a fan of the era of Charlemagne and his brother Warren was a considerable student of French history, as a secondary derivation one could suggest *Telmar* to be a clever reversal of Charles Martel, the grandfather of Charlemagne who won the battle of Tours in 732. But that seems to me a bit fanciful.

Another cleverly presented name is the author of Caspian's grammar text, Pulverulentus Siccus. *Pulverulent* is a seventeenth-century English word, obsolete today, meaning "dusty." Its Latin root is exactly the form Lewis uses here for the first name. *Siccus* takes the forms *siccity* and *siccative* in English, both words dating from around 1500. The *Oxford English Dictionary* cites Sir Thomas Browne as the reference for *siccity,* presumably from *Religio Medici,* a seventeenth-century work Lewis knew well. In either English form, or in its French form, *siccus,* which Lewis uses here, means "dry"; thus the author of the grammar text, Pulverulentus Siccus, is literally "dusty dry," or in the folksy common phrase, as dry as dust. As my occupation, like Lewis's, has caused me to pore over many a grammar book through the decades, I have no difficulty determining why he chose this name!

For the trip to the castle tower where Caspian will learn about his identity, Lewis specifies that Caspian and Dr. Cornelius are clad in buskins "so that they made almost no noise" (44). The word is well chosen on both the literary and practical levels, for a buskin is a leathery shoe (possibly derived from *buckskin*) that would muffle footsteps, and in addition it carries theatrical overtones. In the theater world the buskin has traditionally been associated with serious drama (as opposed to the sock for comedy), and with the suspense and significance of the upcoming scene, Lewis is preparing us symbolically for a moment of serious drama.

Caspian and Dr. Cornelius approach the castle's central tower and begin to climb the "dark winding stair," which is "long and steep," up to the roof. Most of Lewis's everyday world found its way into his books in one form or another, and thus it's interesting to note the description by Douglas Gresham (Lewis's stepson) of the tower in the section of Oxford (Magdalen College) where Lewis taught: "a dark narrow spiral staircase that seemed to go on forever" (Lewis, *Letters to Children* 1).

On the castle roof Dr. Cornelius tells Caspian of Aslan's people, the Old Narnians, who have been overcome by the Telmarines. This bears some resemblance to the Jews and Gentiles of Jesus' day, especially in regard to Dr. Cornelius himself. He is a half dwarf and says that true dwarfs "would despise me and call me a traitor" (48), which parallels the position of the Samaritans, the Jewish-Gentile mix, at the time of Christ.

Caspian continues his studies, which are medieval ones. Lewis includes a significant sentence about one field of study which Caspian is not taught: "Of Navigation ('Which is a noble and heroical art,' said the Doctor) he was taught nothing, because King Miraz disapproved of ships and the sea" (53). Lewis himself loved the sea, and throughout the Chronicles characters' feelings about the sea are a clear indication of whether Lewis approved of them or not. Among the numerous examples besides this one, we note later in *Caspian* how the Telmarines (who originally came from seafaring stock) have grown to fear the water, and in *Treader* we will see that one of the telltale differences between the positively portrayed Pevensies and their evil cousin Eustace is that Eustace gets seasick while the Pevensies have their sea legs.

Soon afterward Caspian learns that his uncle, Miraz, has gained the throne by murdering his father, a plot feature derived from *Hamlet.* Just as Hamlet escapes his uncle Claudius's murder plot, so Caspian escapes Miraz's, and he makes his way with several Narnians to the place now known as Aslan's How. This is the former site of the Stone Table, hence the site of Aslan's death, and fittingly, a *how* (from Middle English, originating from Old Norse) is a "burial mound."

The Pevensie children, meanwhile, have learned these details from Trumpkin, who had originally treated them in a cavalier and patronizing manner, calling them "dear little friends." After their various skills are displayed, the dwarf gets his comeuppance from Edmund, who keeps referring to him needlingly as "Our Dear Little Friend." Lewis grew up in a family where nicknames abounded; even into college his brother Warren referred to him in letters as

"It." Among friends, C. S. Lewis was always called "Jack"; his brother Warren was familiarly known as "Warnie."

Teased beyond endurance, Trumpkin says to Edmund, "No more of that, your Majesty, if you love me" (105). Except for slight modernization of language, this is virtually a direct quote of Falstaff's plea when being teased by Prince Hal in the famous "buckram" episode of Shakespeare's *Henry IV, Part 1* (2.4.283): "Ah, no more of that, Hal, and thou lovest me!" (Shakespeare 861).

The Pevensie children are led on their next stage of the journey by Lucy, who has more faith in Aslan than anyone else in the group. She can see Aslan when the others cannot; thus they are required to walk by faith and not by sight. Finally the Pevensies and Trumpkin arrive at Aslan's "party," a wild dance and celebration including figures the children have not met before. One of them, Bromios, looks according to Edmund as though he might do "absolutely anything." "Bromios" is another name for Dionysus, the Greek god of wine and reveling. Two other Greek gods of wine, Bacchus and Silenus, attend the party as well. Susan and Lucy agree at the end of chapter 11 that they wouldn't feel safe among Bacchus and his colleagues "if we'd met them without Aslan" (154). In other words, without the governance and discipline of Christianity, drinking can be dangerous.

Peter, Edmund, and Trumpkin arrive at Caspian's cave just in time to fight Nikabrik, a Hag, and a Wer-Wolf, which Lewis spells this way to emphasize the Anglo-Saxon origin of the word. *Wer* is Anglo-Saxon for man; hence a werewolf is a man-wolf. The werewolf was in the process of turning from a man into a wolf at the moment he was killed. Significantly, Peter notes that the creature has a "wolf's head and man's body" (167). Just as in *Lion,* the fact that the head has become beast while the body is human shows that the creature allows passion to rule over reason, making it join the forces of evil.

Peter Pevensie, as High King, decides to challenge Miraz to single combat. It would be impossible to determine an individual source for this plot device, since the concept of single combat between onlooking armies occurs in so many cultural traditions:

Greek/Trojan (Patroclus and Hector), Hebrew/Philistine (David and Goliath), and Persian (Sohrab and Rustum), for instance. A less-known parallel to contemporary readers, but one certainly familiar to Lewis, was the German/Anglo-Saxon tradition. H. R. Ellis Davidson describes the heritage this way: "Records from the early history of the Germans have many references to single combat between two champions, while behind them the opposing armies waited and watched. The spirit of such a combat is well expressed in the eighth century by Paul the deacon, who wrote in a history of the Lombards: 'See how many people there are on both sides! What need is there that so great a multitude perish? Let us join, he and I, in single combat'" (58).

The formal challenge Peter issues to Miraz provides Lewis a pleasing opportunity to display his linguistic and historical background. Peter's reminder to Dr. Cornelius to spell "abominable" with an *h* is really Lewis's reminder to readers that the word was spelled that way in English from 1300 to 1650. Specifically, the reminder is a parallel to an incident in Shakespeare's most language-focused play, *Love's Labor's Lost*. In 5.1.24, Holofernes is lamenting Nathaniel's poor pronunciation, saying, "This is abhominable— which he would call abominable." Thus Peter's caution to include the *h* is a warning not to come across as language-flawed bumpkins in writing the challenge.

The *monomachy* to which Miraz is challenged is the sixteenth-century word for "duel." Edmund's titles, it will be noticed, are listed in the traditional British fashion of descending order: king, duke, count, and knight. Finally, Lewis uses the Anglo-Saxon (earlier, Hebrew and Latin) tradition of reign dating, giving the challenge "in the first year of Caspian Tenth of Narnia" (173). This, it should be noticed, additionally serves to annoy Miraz by indicating that his reign is over and Caspian's has begun; Lewis's word choices generally manage to further the plot and please the intellect simultaneously.

The challenge is delivered to Miraz's lords, Glozelle and Sopespian. Glozelle fashions a plan to deceive Miraz into accepting the challenge; *gloze* in Middle English means to flatter or deceive.

Glozelle's reason for deceit, that he and Sopespian put Miraz on the throne and have been repaid with ingratitude, parallels the plot of *Henry IV, Part 1*, where Worcester and Hotspur, two of the key leaders in overthrowing Richard II and placing Henry IV on the throne, confer in complaint over Henry's supposed ingratitude toward them. After the Battle of Beruna near the river town by that name (*berun* being a sixteenth-century word meaning "to run or flow around"), Aslan appears and begins working miracles. In *Lion*, Lewis was able to present only the death and resurrection of Christ; in *Caspian*, he fills in some gaps from the life. The freeing of the animals parallels Christ's mission as given in Luke 4:18b: "to heal the brokenhearted, to preach deliverance to the captives, and recovering of sight to the blind, to set at liberty them that are bruised." In the Narnian version, sad old donkeys become young and joyous, horses no longer have to pull carts, and dogs become unchained. In other parallel events evil boys turn into pigs, similar to the casting of the demons into swine in the fifth chapter of Mark; an old woman is healed, similar to several of the healing miracles in the Gospels; and water is turned into wine, just as in Christ's first New Testament miracle (John 2:1–11). Thus the post-temptation life of Christ is fairly amply covered in the first two Chronicles. In the remaining books, when Aslan's actions have a biblical parallel, they generally, with few and brief exceptions, come from some portion of the Bible besides the Gospels.

As you might expect by now, however, not all of Aslan's miracles have their sources in the Bible. Lewis never stuck to one source when he could possibly mix in more. The miracle of the child-beating man turning into a tree (195) is unlike anything biblical, but it parallels numerous episodes from Ovid's *Metamorphoses*, the mythological collection that for centuries was used by Latin teachers in British schools to improve their students' grammar and vocabulary. One of the most famous of Ovid's stories concerns the lust of Apollo for Daphne. When he pursued her and she feared rape, she prayed to her father Peneus (a river god), and he turned her into a laurel tree. Lewis, of course, reverses the metamorphosis; in *Caspian* the chaser turns into a tree, not the chased. When Lewis alters sources in his Narnian books, he tends to alter them in a direction that will serve justice better. Since most people consider becoming a tree a step down from being human, he uses the metamorphosis in this chapter of *Caspian* as a fitting punishment. Since the man beats the boy with a piece of wood, he turns into wood himself.

One final allusion from *Caspian* I will comment upon more than its novel importance merits, for it is so characterically Lewisian. The book's final chapter mentions a feast in which everyone participates, both flora and fauna. If it's a banquet for everyone, however, how can the trees enjoy soil richer than their normal fare? Lewis solves this problem by having a group of moles bring special dirt to the trees as their portion of the feast. The leader of the moles, he has casually noted earlier, is named Clodsley Shovel. The name makes linguistic sense; moles shovel up clods. And so I used to think that was the entire story.

Then some years ago I was reading a book of seventeenth-century British history. The book described the growth of British naval power during the century and mentioned some of the leading commanders. The commander of the British navy in the 1690s, it noted, was named (believe it or not) Cloudesley Shovel. And I remember laughing out loud and shouting in delight, "That's Clodsley Shovel! That's where Lewis got the name!" My enjoyment of Clodsley Shovel's name was much greater than if Lewis had named the mole leader, say, Spadesley Dirt, or some other name that used linguistics but didn't bring in the historical reference.

And that brings up an important point. Lewis expected at least some readers to recognize his allusions and gain added pleasure from them. He expected educated adults to pick up on the allusions right away; he expected children to recognize more of the allusions as they continued their education. When Walter Hooper came during the last year of Lewis's life to visit and provide secretarial help, he wanted to understand Lewis's daily schedule. So one day shortly after they started working together, he asked, "Do you take a nap in the afternoons?"

Lewis wittily answered, "No—but sometimes a nap takes me!" It's a clever response but not an original one. Dr. Sam Johnson, one of the most important figures in eighteenth-century British literature, had given the same answer to the same question two hundred years earlier, when future biographer James Boswell began spending time with him. Lewis did not explain to Hooper that the line was unoriginal; Hooper was an educated man, so Lewis assumed Hooper had to recognize the line. How could any educated man not know the prime witticisms of Dr. Johnson?

Did Lewis really make these kinds of assumptions about the literary knowledge of his readers? The best way to determine that is to move from his children's fiction to his adult religious nonfiction, written for a general audience. *Mere Christianity,* the adult book Lewis is today most famous for in the U.S., stemmed from his radio talks to a general audience. In the preface to that book, which he wrote with a general audience in mind, Lewis noted that his theological beliefs were basically standard Anglican views. To indicate this, he said of his views: "To quote Uncle Toby: 'They are written in the Common-Prayer Book.'" Lewis thinks his readers, at least some of them, will nod their heads in recognition at the mention of Uncle Toby—one of the three main characters in Laurence Sterne's obscure 1761 novel, *Tristram Shandy.* He expects us to get the references, or at least a good portion of them.

This lengthy digression provides another good reason, then, to have a book explaining the references and allusions—the author of the Chronicles expects us to get them. He expects adults to get (at least part of) them on a first reading, and kids to understand them as they mature and read more. So to read the books as Lewis expected them to be read, we need to recognize the allusions. If we don't, we miss some important features of Lewis's personality, especially his fine sense of humor. He wants us to enjoy fully the name Clodsley Shovel!

# CHAPTER 4

# "The Way to Aslan's Country": Allusions in *The Voyage of the "Dawn Treader"*

The famous first line of *The Voyage of the "Dawn Treader"* contains an oblique personal reference: "There was a boy named Eustace Clarence Scrubb, and he almost deserved it" (1). Lewis knew personally the nuisance of having an odd name, having himself been christened Clive Staples; he is the only major British author seemingly named for office supplies. His distaste for the name became clear during his preschool days, when he announced to the family that he was henceforward to be called "Jack," a nickname he retained thereafter. This distaste for "Clive Staples" remained with Lewis for the rest of his life because each of his books, whether academic or popular, identified his first two names by initials only.

A likely source for the name *Eustace* was Lewis's academic friend E. M. W. Tillyard, as he was known on book covers. Tillyard's full name was Eustace Mandeville Wetenhall Tillyard, and he didn't deserve it, being a courteous scholar. Tillyard and Lewis knew each other well, since they taught English together at Oxford for several years and published together a literary dispute, *The Personal Heresy*. (In an interesting parallel, they both moved from Oxford to Cambridge in their fifties.) It certainly seems reasonable that the two men on some occasion found they shared annoyance at their given names.

Scrubb's middle name, Clarence, was a name in disfavor among the British for many decades. Perhaps this came from the ignoble death of George, Duke of Clarence, in the fifteenth century. According to legend, which may be true, he drowned in a "butt of malmsey" (cask of sweet wine). Whether this be the source of its disfavor or not, "Clarence" became unpopular. As is noted in *Stories behind Everyday Things,* the names "Clarence and Harvey inevitably draw ridicule. In 1965 the much-maligned Harveys organized to stop TV commercials from presenting Harvey as a bumbling boor. Clarences had done the same decades earlier, when the mere mention of the name drew guffaws from vaudeville audiences" (229).

While on the subject of names, we should note that *Treader* is the first book in the series to give the last name of Peter, Susan, Edmund, and Lucy; they are the Pevensie children. To most American readers, this word means nothing, but it is part of one of the most famous events in English history. In 1066, Harold took over as king of England, but William of Normandy believed the crown should belong to him. He and his supporters landed on the southeastern shore of England and, in October 1066, won a major battle at Hastings, gaining for William the crown and the title of "William the Conqueror."

How does this impact Narnia? When William and his ships crossed the English Channel, the village where they landed, their point of entry into the realm of England, was called Pevensey. (Pevensey for an educated British audience might have the same historical ring of familiarity that Bunker Hill would for Americans.) Similarly, the Pevensie children are in the Chronicles the point of entry from our world into the realm of Narnia.

The three visitors from Earth eventually join Caspian and learn of his journey to this point. He has passed up a potential opportunity to marry the Duke of Galma's daughter because she "squints, and has freckles" (17). This is reminiscent of Jack Absolute's imagined description of Lydia Languish in Richard Sheridan's eighteenth-century comedy *The Rivals.* In an effort to convince his father that he is willing to marry any lady, however unattractive, Jack puzzles over the name of Languish a few moments before commenting in 3.1.54, "She squints, don't she? A little red-haired girl?" The description is clearly an unappealing one, as his father, Sir Anthony, responds with, "Squints? A red-haired girl? Zounds! no" (Sheridan 54–55). Red hair is, or course, frequently associated with freckles, and Lewis uses the description for humorous effect, as it is used here (and later as well) in *The Rivals*. A more direct use of squinting in a negative sense comes from William Wycherley's seventeenth-century comedy *The Plain Dealer,* 2.1, in which Olivia rhetorically asks, "Can anyone be called beautiful that squints?" (Wycherley 918). So in British literature, squinting has a traditional association with unattractiveness.

After leaving Galma, the Dawn Treader sails to Terebinthia. Lewis, the renowned medieval scholar, naturally knew that *terebinth* was Middle English for the tree used in the Middle Ages to produce turpentine.

We learn a few pages later that Eustace comes from Cambridge. Lewis at the time of writing *Treader* was still Oxfordian, and since there is a good-natured rivalry between the two major British universities, it seems probable that having the unpleasant Eustace hail from Cambridge is a quiet piece of Oxfordian humor. (Clearly Lewis harbored no genuine resentment against Cambridge; not only did he later move there, but his space trilogy hero, Ransom, hails from Cambridge.)

Having learned that he is apparently to be in Narnia for an extended period of time, Eustace "at once got out a little black notebook and a pencil and started to keep a diary" (24). In some ways the preconversion Eustace mirrors (in exaggerated form) the preconversion Lewis, and it is worth noting here that the preconversion Lewis also kept a diary. After becoming a Christian, Lewis seemed somewhat embarrassed by the valuation on one's own thoughts implied by keeping a diary and remarked that the only valuable thing about the experience was a greater appreciation for the skills of eighteenth-century biographer and journal-keeper James Boswell.

*Treader* contains ten diary entries for Eustace before his "baptism," none after, and it seems likely that Eustace, like Lewis, found other, more outward-looking things to focus upon after that point.

The ostensible purpose of the journey is to find seven lords of Narnia who had left several years earlier during a time of Narnian unrest. The first one they meet is Lord Bern, who helps them overthrow the rule of Gumpas on the Lone Islands by putting on armor, attacking the sentry, turning over a castle table, and helping to plan the entire campaign. He is the only one of the seven lords who engages in any sort of warlike activity in the book—a suitable characteristic because, according to the *Oxford English Dictionary*, *berne* is a sixteenth-century word meaning "warrior."

The parallel between Bern's name and an Old English word does not mean a similar parallel can be found for each of the lords; after all, as Freud is famous for allegedly noting, sometimes a cigar is just a cigar, and sometimes a name is just a name. Lewis delighted in what seventeenth-century poet Robert Herrick called "sweet disorder," a characteristic that fellow Inkling-member J. R. R. Tolkien considered a severe writing flaw. Had Tolkien written *Treader*, all the seven lords would have had parallels to their names, or none would have. Lewis, ever the model of inconsistency, would sometimes pick names for linguistic echoes, sometimes for literary reasons, and sometimes simply because he liked the sounds the letters made.

Lord Bern has for some time wanted to end the slave trade with Calormen, a country south of Narnia. It is a hot, desert country, as the Spanish and Latin *calor* (hot) would indicate. To some extent the Calormenes, as they are called, seem modeled after Lewis's idea of the Muslims in medieval literature: a "wise, wealthy, courteous, cruel, and ancient people" (50). The Calormen monetary unit is the crescent, and a crescent (moon) is a traditional symbol of Islam, as the flags of Pakistan, Algeria, and Turkey reveal. The smaller monetary unit, the minim, at first seems to be simply a shortened form of *minimum* or *minimal*, but *minim* was an actual word in Renaissance times, used in 1592 to mean "the smallest possible portion."

The Narnian crew prepares to leave the Lone Islands and asks about eastward lands but hears only "wild stories of headless men, floating islands, waterspouts, and a fire that burned along the water" (52). The first and third of these were commonplace stories from the travel books Renaissance readers perused so eagerly; Lewis had already used the second concept effectively in *Perelandra*; the fourth item may have been a Renaissance travel-book feature as well.

The Narnian party lands on what later becomes known as Dragon Island, and Eustace decides to get away for a while, slipping down "a slide of loose stones (scree, they call it)" (66). The term is an eighteenth-century word, with the meaning Lewis indicates; he clearly goes out of his way to use it, and I suspect the reason is that *scree* derives from Old Norse. Anything old or Norse attracted Lewis; he found the combination irresistible.

Eustace falls asleep on a pile of treasure in a dragon cave. As Lewis notes, "Sleeping on a dragon's hoard with greedy, dragonish thoughts in his heart, he had become a dragon himself" (75). The combination of *heart* with treasure leads one directly to Matthew 6:21: "For where your treasure is, there will your heart be also." Lewis was ever fascinated by possibilities of interior thought shaping external appearance; in *The Screwtape Letters,* for instance, Screwtape's anger causes him inadvertently to become a centipede, and in *The Great Divorce* the failure of the spirits' thoughts to match reality causes them to remain insubstantial.

A more direct source for the transmutation is Norse mythology, which traditionally associates treasure with dragons. In the *Prose Edda,* for instance, when Fafnir wanted to guard his treasure, he "turned himself into a dragon and lay down on the gold" (Sturluson 112). Fafnir died "crawling on his way down to the water" (112), which of course is where Eustace finds the dragon that preceded him. The whole association of men and dragons and treasure is more clearly explained by H. R. Ellis Davidson: "Both in England and Scandinavia the dragon came to be regarded as the guardian of the grave mound, watching over its treasures. Sometimes it is implied that he is to be identified with the dead man buried in the mound, and in some of the late legendary sagas it is said that a man after death became a dragon and guarded the treasure which he had taken into the howe with him" (161).

You will notice that the last line of this source contains the word *how* (here spelled *howe*), meaning "burial mound," which Lewis uses elsewhere in the Chronicles: "Aslan's How" is the site where Aslan was sacrificed in *Lion*.

When Eustace becomes imprisoned in a dragon body, his great emotional supporter is Reepicheep, who continually explains that "what had happened to Eustace was a striking illustration of the turn of Fortune's wheel" (84). The turning of Fortune's wheel is such a medieval/Renaissance commonplace one hesitates to point out a specific source. Yet, although Lewis knew the concept from dozens of places, one he would have valued perhaps most highly would have been Boethius's *The Consolation of Philosophy*. Boethius was a Roman nobleman who lived in the early 500s under the emperor Theodoric. Being falsely accused of treason, Boethius spent much of his prison sentence writing in *The Consolation* about how having a philosophical attitude can help one deal calmly with the vicissitudes of life. He was a major influence on European writers for the next thousand years; in fact, Lewis lectured at Cambridge on the effect of Boethius on medieval and Renaissance writers. Boethius has a substantial section on the unpredictability of Fortune's wheel, noting that "when Fortune turns her wheel with her proud right hand, she is . . . unpredictable" (23). Appropriately, considering the title of Boethius's work, Reepicheep is using this concept to console Eustace with philosophy.

The justly famous "baptism" scene, wherein Aslan finally skins Eustace and tosses him into a pool, has a variety of theological implications and parallels. Aslan leads Eustace to a paradisal mountaintop garden with "trees and fruit and everything" (88). The garden holds a marble bath with a "bubbling" well at the bottom of it. According to the Didache, a valuable collection of apostolic practice dating from around the early second century, early Christians preferred to baptize people in "living" water, meaning bubbling or running water, as opposed to the contemporary practice of still water in baptisteries. The unusual feature of Aslan's baptistery, where living water comes up from a well rather than a spring as one might expect, issues from the biblical story of the Samaritan woman at the well, to whom Christ offers "living water" (here with a different meaning) from "a well of water springing up into everlasting life" (John 4:10b, 14b). A literary source (adored by Lewis) in which living water issues from a well is Edmund Spenser's sixteenth-century epic poem *The Faerie Queene* 1.2.43, in which the lost spirits say to the Red Crosse Knight that they will be misshapen "till we be bathed in a living well" (Spenser 29).

Aslan tells Eustace to "undress" before entering the water, implying that repentance comes before baptism. Lewis said little about baptism in his nonfiction writings, perceiving it as an issue likely to divide Christians rather than promote "mere Christianity." It is interesting, however, that the chronological placement of repentance before baptism opposes standard Anglican practice regarding infant baptism. Perhaps Lewis saw Eustace as a prototypical adult convert who would have a change of heart before undergoing the sacrament.

Eustace first scratches off his scales, or sins, and then his whole skin, or sinful self. Despite several sheddings of skin, however, he is unable to change himself, thereby making one of Lewis's favorite theological points from his adult nonfiction, that Christianity is not simply a matter of self-improvement but of becoming something entirely different. This thought can be seen clearly in *Mere Christianity*: "It may be hard for an egg to turn into a bird; it would be a jolly sight harder for it to learn to fly while remaining an egg" (169). When Eustace comes up out of the water, he has changed from a dragon into a boy, externally showing his alteration and literally exemplifying 2 Corinthians 5:17a: "Therefore if any man be in Christ, he is a new creature."

The Narnian ship continues to push eastward, narrowly escaping the Sea Serpent (which Lewis could have pulled from numberless

sources) and arriving at the island where a pool of water turns everything that enters it into gold. Presumably all stories like this stem at
least partially from the legend of King Midas. The discovery of the
gold pool immediately causes division among the travelers, remind-
ing us of the famous Scripture that "the love of money is the root of
all evil" (1 Tim. 6:10). Interestingly, the much less famous preceding
verse may also play a role in this scene. It says, "But they that will be
rich fall into temptation and a snare . . . which drown[s] men in
destruction." When Edmund suddenly warns everyone back, it is
because of the risk of falling into the gold pool, which can drown
them in destruction—an interesting piece of wordplay, if this was
Lewis's intention.

Aslan appears at the moment of conflict, seen first by Lucy (as
usual). When he arrives, Lewis cleverly uses atmospheric conditions
to show him as brighter (and symbolically more powerful) than the
gold, for while the gold shone under the brightness of the sun, Aslan
shines "though the sun had in fact gone in" (107). Lewis is using
various Scriptures, particularly in Revelation, that indicate how
Christ takes the place of the sun. Revelation 21:23, speaking of the
new Jerusalem, says, "And the city had no need of the sun, neither
of the moon, to shine in it: for . . . the Lamb is the light thereof."
And since, as Matthew 6:24 comments, "Ye cannot serve God and
Mammon [riches]," after Aslan makes his appearance, the quarrel is
forgotten and the group converses amicably again.

Lewis includes in this section an interesting and subtle piece of
commentary on the Bible. After the appearance of Aslan on the gold-
water island, a pair of sentences are given to a later recounting of his
appearance. "In describing the scene Lucy said afterwards, 'He was
the size of an elephant,' though at another time she only said, 'The
size of a carthorse.' But it was not the size that mattered" (107–8).

Since Lucy is here describing (after the fact) details of an experience with Aslan, she is doing what in our world would be the
equivalent of writing Scripture. She in many ways parallels the apostle John, as noted previously, and John wrote five books of the New
Testament. As an elephant and a carthorse are not the same size, by

a considerable margin, one of her descriptions must have been erroneous. But Lewis notes that the exact size didn't matter since it was clearly Aslan in either case.

This appears to be a quiet blow against inerrancy, a doctrine that Lewis disbelieved in and wrote against (privately, so as not to divide Christendom) more than once. One presentation of his views can be found in a May 7, 1959, letter to Clyde Kilby (numbers refer to six points he has just listed against inerrancy):

> It seems to me that 2 and 4 rule out the view that
> every statement in scripture must be *historical* truth. . . .
> [This], I think, rules out the view that any one passage
> taken in isolation can be assumed to be inerrant in exactly
> the same sense as any other, e.g., that the numbers of O.T.
> armies (which in view of the size of the country, if true,
> involve continuous miracle) are statistically correct
> because the story of the resurrection is historically correct. (*Letters* 480, emphasis his)

Clearly, Lewis's comment about Lucy's description of Aslan parallels this view. He allows her to be mistaken but emphasizes that the important point is that it genuinely was Aslan who appeared. It is characteristic of Lewis to make his point in such a subtle and sophisticated way to avoid distressing people, especially children, who may have been taught other views.

Even though the voyagers do not learn the name of the lord in the gold pool till later, for chronological clarity I will cover him here. They learn in a subsequent chapter that the lord resting at the bottom of the pool is Restimar. Since *mar,* as noted earlier, is Latin for "a body of water," and *i'* is the abbreviated Elizabethan form of *in,* one can deduce that *Restimar* is a playful name for one who "rests in a body of water." What marvelous cleverness!

The next island the *Dawn Treader* visits, the land of the Dufflepuds, has a number of similarities to the island Prospero rules in Shakespeare's *The Tempest.* In each case the island is "the property of a great magician" who has servants. The magician has told the servants "to do something we didn't like" (117). The magician on

Dufflepud Island naps in the afternoons, and, according to Caliban, "'tis a custom with [Prospero] / I' th' afternoon to sleep" (3.2.87–88). And of course each island contains a book of powerful spells.

In discussing the possible appearance of the invisible Dufflepuds, Eustace suggests to Edmund that the creatures might be like "huge grasshoppers" (124). At the turn of the century, H. G. Wells was a chief perpetrator of the "alien as insect" science fiction story, and Lewis was a genuine Wells fan, as he comments in the introductory note to *Out of the Silent Planet*. Edmund asks Eustace not to mention the idea of grasshoppers to Lucy because she is "not too keen on insects; specially big ones" (124). Here Lucy is a literary substitute for Lewis, who was somewhat fearful of insects throughout his life. In "On Three Ways of Writing for Children," he noted, "none of my fears came from fairy tales. Giant insects were my specialty" (*Of Other Worlds* 30).

Lewis includes a second Shakespearean reference in the same chapter when Lucy is flipping through a book of spells; he mentions the book contains a spell on "how to give a man an ass's head" (as they did to poor Bottom). Lewis was quite familiar with *A Midsummer Night's Dream,* and the character he liked best from the play may well have been Bottom the weaver. One of Lewis's favorite pieces of wordplay, in fact, was about an all-female production of the play; he said it was the first time he had ever seen a female Bottom.

Lucy proceeds further into the book of spells and discovers the enchantment to make a woman the most beautiful in the world. She sees images of her beauty causing a great war, and the reader is readily reminded of *The Iliad,* where the beauty of Helen of Troy caused a ten-year war between the Greeks and the Trojans. The book of spells contains a lovely story, but when Lucy tries to reread it, she discovers that the pages only turn forward, meaning that she cannot repeat the experience. This is similar to the concept Lewis had earlier used in *Perelandra,* where Ransom does not immediately repeat the bubble tree and red-heart berry experiences. Here is the bubble-tree version: "To repeat a pleasure so intense and almost so spiritual seemed an obvious thing to do. . . . But for whatever cause, it appeared to him better not to taste again. Perhaps the experience had been so complete that repetition would be a vulgarity—like asking to hear the same symphony twice in a day" (*Perelandra* 42–43). In one respect the episodes contrast, in that Ransom (an older and wiser character) chooses not to repeat his experiences, whereas Lucy tries to but is prevented from doing so.

When she tries to remember the story, she can only recall that it "was about a cup and sword and a tree and a green hill" (133). The references seem to imply that the story is about the crucifixion: the cup would represent the Holy Grail, which caught the blood of Christ on the cross (or in other versions was the cup used at the Last Supper); the tree would represent the cross, which is frequently in biblical and patristic literature referred to as a tree; and the green hill would refer to Calvary, which is traditionally described in hymns and commentaries as a hill, and sometimes specifically as a green hill, as in Cecil Alexander's nineteenth-century hymn, "On a Green Hill Far Away." The significance of the sword is more elusive. The description of Jesus' arrest in Matthew 26:47–55 contains five references to swords in a nine-verse section, but each individual mention seems fairly minor compared to the references for the other story items (Holy Grail, cross, and Calvary). Possibly the sword is a subtle reference to Christ/Aslan himself, since Ephesians 6:17 refers to "the word of God" as a sword, and in John 1:1 Christ is called the Word. Or perhaps the story sword is simply a collective reference to the swords of Matthew 26. Aside from the objects involved, the crucifixion would be a likely guess for the story anyway; it clearly seems to involve Aslan and be of significance, since he says to Lucy that he will be talking with her about it "for years and years" (136).

Lucy discusses with the magician the plight of the Dufflepuds who have been, as they put it, uglified. The word comes from *Alice in Wonderland*, where the Mock Turtle tells Alice the four mathematical processes—"Ambition, Distraction, Uglification, and Derision" (Carroll 76). Three of those terms were already words;

*uglification* was coined by Carroll. Lewis himself was a coiner of words, as can be seen on the very next page, where we find a list of the magician's instruments, such as astrolabes and theodolinds, which are indeed Renaissance surveying and astronomical instruments. But another of the instruments, the choriambus, is an obscure metric foot from Greek poetry (accented syllable, two unaccented, accented), and the *poesimeter* is not a word at all, though the formation would indicate it is an instrument for measuring poetry. Lewis enjoyed playfulness in other writers, especially wordplay, and frequently engaged in it himself. And once again we see his consistent inconsistency: some of the words are actual Elizabethan words that fit the topic, one is an Elizabethan word that doesn't fit the topic, and one is a word Lewis creates for himself. Presumably Tolkien, upon reading this paragraph, would have rolled his eyes in disgust.

The mariners travel next to Dark Island, where nightmares come true. Lewis himself struggled painfully with nightmares for much of his life. Lucy asks Aslan to rescue them, engaging in a form of prayer, and in answer she sees what first looks like a cross and eventually turns out to be an albatross. The cross shape is an obvious Christian symbol; the albatross is the traditional good-luck bird of the sea, most familiar to us in literature from Coleridge's *The Rime of the Ancient Mariner*. The albatross circles three times, in fine Trinitarian fashion, then leads the ship in a starboard direction, which means toward the right-hand side. The right side is always the favored one in both Christian culture (the parable of the sheep and the goats, where the saved go to the right and the lost to the left) and pagan culture (as with the Romans, for whom right was *dexter* and left was *sinister*).

The ship continues eastward, the direction of holiness for Renaissance European cultures since Jerusalem was in the East. John Donne's splendid poem "Good-Friday 1613, Riding Westward" is a typical work displaying the European idea that at holy times one should be traveling toward, looking toward, or at least thinking about, the East. The first sign that they are nearing Aslan's country is the "crimson and purple" skies, the two traditional colors of royalty (163).

The first piece of land they encounter in the environs of Aslan's country is the island where three men perpetually sleep at a sacramental banqueting place called Aslan's Table. *Treader* is the most sacramentally oriented of the Chronicles. Eustace's undragoning clearly emblemizes baptism, and Lucy had observed that the magician on the island of the Dufflepuds "drank only wine and ate only bread" (139). In this chapter Aslan's Table parallels the Eucharist, sometimes known in Protestant circles as the Lord's table. The Knife of Stone which lies on the table, being the instrument that killed Aslan, stands for the cross. First Corinthians 11:26b says the purpose of meeting at the Lord's table is to "shew [show] the Lord's death till he come." It is noteworthy that when the three lords of Narnia arrived at the table, they did not recognize what it meant and failed to reverence it properly, even to the extent of one of them grabbing hold of the Knife of Stone to fight with his comrades. When that happened, they all fell asleep. Interestingly, the Eucharist passage in 1 Corinthians 11 says that some people will approach the Lord's table inappropriately, "not discerning the Lord's body. For this cause many are weak and sickly among you, and many sleep" (29b–30). The metaphorical sleep of 1 Corinthians has here become a physical sleep.

When the sun rises over Aslan's Table, symbolizing Christ's presence, thousands of large birds come to cover everything. They have marked similarities to traditional descriptions of angels, being large, white, flying, singing creatures that speak in "a language which no one knew" (178). This last reminds one of the "tongues . . . of angels" of 1 Corinthians 13:1. The section contains a striking parallel to Isaiah 6, where an angel takes a live coal and "laid it upon my [Isaiah's] mouth" (7a). In the *Treader* passage, one of the birds takes what appears to be "a little live coal" and "the bird laid it in the old Man's mouth" (178).

The Old Man, Ramandu, is a "retired" star, as the children charmingly put it. He informs the voyagers that Coriakin, the magician ruling the Dufflepuds, is a fallen star. The idea of stars being able to fall comes from Isaiah 14:12a: "How art thou fallen from heaven, O Lucifer, son of the morning." Lucifer is traditionally taken to refer to Satan; the alternate King James translation of *Lucifer* is "day star." Ramandu tells the mariners that to break the sleeping enchantment they must sail to "the World's End." That is a phrase that Lewis loved for years, having borrowed it from William Morris's novel *The Well at the World's End.* As Lewis put it in *On Stories, "The Well at the World's End*—can a man write a story to that title?" (17).

At the end of *Treader,* after Reepicheep has flung his sword into the sea in a gesture reminiscent of the passing of King Arthur, the Pevensies and Eustace enter Aslan's country. There Aslan himself greets them in the form of a Lamb, echoing numerous biblical descriptions of Christ (e.g., John 1:36) as the Lamb of God. The Lamb invites them to a fish breakfast, just as Christ prepares a fish breakfast for the apostles in John 21.

That allusion is developed further in the conversation Lucy and Aslan have after the meal. When Aslan tells Lucy she can never return to Narnia, for her a sort of emotional death, she asks whether Eustace will ever return. Aslan responds, "Do you really need to know that?" (216). In the twenty-first chapter of the book of John, the apostle Peter is told by Christ about his future martyrdom. When Peter then asks what will happen to John, Christ replies, "If I will that he tarry till I come, what is that to thee?" (John 21:22b).

It is worth noting in this regard that, although Lucy in the Chronicles generally parallels the apostle John from the Gospels, here in a biblical episode featuring John and Peter, she parallels Peter. This shows again that Lewis made no effort—and indeed, had no desire—to be consistent regarding his allusions. Such inconsistency may be a reason Lewis steadfastly refused to label his novels allegorical.

A supplementary reason, if one were needed, also comes into play with the closing of *Treader.* Aslan tells the children that the way into his country from theirs is over a river, clearly meaning they will have to die first. In pagan tradition this river is the Styx; in Christian hymns and spirituals, it's the river Jordan. Since repeatedly Lewis's terms have multiple meanings, it's preferable to say the books contain allegorical elements rather than to label each novel an allegory.

CHAPTER 5

# "The Healing of Harms": Allusions in *The Silver Chair*

*The Silver Chair* opens and closes with biographical elements and includes several borrowings from Lewis's life and writings in the middle, making it overall the most personal of the Chronicles. The novel begins with Jill Pole crying at her school. Lewis says he is going to say "as little as possible" (1) about the school, but with Lewis's strong feelings on that subject, it is never possible for him to say as little as possible. In this case he continues griping about schools in general and Jill's school in particular for another seven sentences. One of the problems with Jill's school, in Lewis's judgment, is that it is coeducational. Preferring the old-fashioned term (as usual), he calls it "mixed," adding, "some said it was not nearly so mixed as the minds of the people who ran it" (1). *Some* is a euphemism for Lewis. For most of his life, he opposed educating males and females together, primarily, it seems, because he felt it would lead to a weakening of education for males.

One of the clearest examples of his desire to keep males and females from "mixing" in education occurred in 1927, when Oxford was considering whether to limit the number of women who could pursue degrees at the university there. Lewis (age 28) wrote a letter to his brother about the issue which merits excerpting: "The Term . . . produced one public event of good omen—the carrying in

Congregation of a Statute limiting the number of wimmen [sic] at Oxford. The appalling danger of our degenerating into a woman's university . . . has thus been staved off" (*Letters* 238). This is Lewis at his pre-Christian worst. As the letter continues, he not only says that he has voted for limiting women but makes clear that he feels it's a vote for "realism," since he and his crowd know what women are really like; a vote to limit women at Oxford comes across as a vote to protect Western civilization. In fairness, this letter was written when Lewis was only twenty-eight, before he became a Christian. But old habits often die hard, even for Christians, and as the opening chapter of *Chair* indicates, Lewis always remained skeptical of coeducation.

The other, and more serious, problem at Jill's school is that the directors "had the idea that boys and girls should be allowed to do what they liked. And unfortunately what ten or fifteen of the biggest boys and girls liked best was bullying the others" (1). As Lewis's autobiography makes painfully clear, he felt he was bullied and made to do the work of the older boys in school more than most— "a marked man," he calls himself (*Surprised* 94). Obviously this would increase his sensitivity toward others, including literary characters, who undergo school bullying.

Jill and Eustace decide, in a clear allusion to prayer, to call on Aslan for rescue from their school situation. To Jill, who is unfamiliar with Aslan, Eustace points out that they can't "make him do things. . . . Really, we can only ask him" (6). This is another instance of "autography," Lewis's borrowing of theological concepts from his adult nonfiction for his children's fiction. Lewis was ever careful, while teaching that prayer can "cause" things, to differentiate it from a sort of magic charm that always "works." Among the pre-*Chair* essays in which he makes this point is "Work and Prayer," published in 1945. There Lewis compares God's responding to petitionary prayer to a school headmaster's saying that some things "are too dangerous to be left to general rules. If you want to do them you must come and make a request and talk over the whole matter with me in my study. And then—we'll see" (*Dock* 107).

When Eustace and Jill enter Narnia, they find themselves on the edge of an incredibly tall cliff, which Jill at first despises Eustace for fearing. The height of the precipice, however, causes her to have fears of her own, and she decides she will "never laugh at anyone for not liking heights again" (12). From a pedagogical point of view, Lewis is encouraging children to have compassion for other children's fears; the reason he selects this particular fear is, as one might guess, his own fear of cliffs. This phobia is not as well-known as his traumas regarding nightmares and insects; one of the places it appears is an August 10, 1953, letter, where he says his two greatest fears are "large spiders and the tops of cliffs" (*Lady* 21).

The "dying of thirst" scene between Jill and Aslan combines so many biblical passages that it would be hard to determine which ones were working in Lewis's mind at which points. Among the many texts informing the scene are John 4:14, where Christ tells the woman at the well he can give her water that will quench her thirst forever; John 6:35, where Christ says anyone who believes in him will never thirst; John 7:37, where Christ tells a crowd that anyone thirsting can come to him and drink; and 1 Corinthians 10:4, in which Christ is called the spiritual drink that satisfied the thirst of the ancient Israelites. Within these contexts Aslan's response "there is no other stream" (17) corresponds to Acts 4:12, which asserts that only through Christ can salvation come.

But the central theological concept for the plot of *Chair* is the emphasis on learning and remembering Scripture. This takes the form of Aslan's giving Jill four "Signs" to remember. (As might be deduced from their spellings, *sign* and *significant* have related Latin roots.) When she has them learned, Aslan tells her to "remember, remember, remember the Signs. Say them to yourself when you wake in the morning and when you lie down at night" (21). The Signs clearly parallel the laws given to Moses on Mount Sinai; Jill also receives her "laws" on a mountain. And Aslan's instructions on how to remember parallel the instructions about the laws given to the Israelites: "And these words, which I command thee this day, shall be in thine heart . . . when thou liest down, and when thou risest up" (Deut. 6:6, 7b).

When Jill and Eustace are reunited at Caspian's castle, they listen to a blind poet telling the historical Narnian epic, *The Horse and His Boy*. Homer, the author of the two major Greek historical poems, *The Iliad* and *The Odyssey*, was traditionally supposed to have been blind. Since Lewis had already written *Horse* but not yet published it, the reference is an inside joke.

The fourth chapter of *Chair* tells of a nighttime gathering of owls and is entitled "A Parliament of Owls." The allusion is to a poem by Chaucer, "Parliament of Fowls"; in addition, *parliament* is the traditional collective noun for owls, thus letting Lewis, in his standard manner, work in literary and linguistic cleverness simultaneously.

The owls say that more than thirty knights have disappeared by going out searching for the lost Prince Rilian, and "at last the King said he was not going to have all the bravest Narnians destroyed in the search for his son" (46). This sounds like the search for the Holy Grail in Arthurian legend. Supposedly the cup from the Last Supper had been transported from Israel to England, so many of the Round Table knights decided to leave Camelot to search for it. In both Thomas Malory's medieval prose piece *Morte D'Arthur* and Alfred Tennyson's epic poem *Idylls of the King*, this episode helped contribute to the breakup of the Round Table through the loss of so many knights on a (mostly) futile quest.

Jill and Eustace hear the story of how Rilian's mother had been killed by a serpent, with Satanic overtones hearkening back to the third chapter of Genesis. In their rescue attempt they join a marshwiggle named Puddleglum, a name Lewis borrowed from sixteenth-century writer John Studley (*Oxford* 256).

According to Walter Hooper, Lewis said that his gardener, Fred Paxford, "served as the model for Puddleglum the marshwiggle" (Green and Hooper 123). Perhaps so. But Lewis had been presenting himself playfully as a Puddleglum-type character many years before writing *Chair*. Puddleglum always puts the worst face on things, yet he says he's the optimist among the marshwiggles: "They all say—I mean, the other wiggles all say—that I'm too flighty; don't take life seriously enough" (64). This characterization bears a remarkable similarity to the persona Lewis adopts in a letter to Owen Barfield on February 8, 1939: "I haven't seen C. W.'s play: it is not like to be at all good. As for Orpheus—again it's no harm trying. If you can't write it, console yourself by reflecting that if you did you w[oul]d have been v[ery] unlikely to get a publisher. I am more and more convinced that there is no future for poetry. Nearly everybody has been ill here: I try to prevent them all croaking and grumbling, but it is hard being the only optimist" (*Letters* 318).

Clearly, this is the voice of Puddleglum. And Lewis is not doing it to imitate Paxford as an inside joke for Barfield; there is no mention of Paxford in the letter and no verbal equivalent of a wink or grin (such as Lewis uses in making fun of his father in letters to his brother). At this date, if Barfield knew Paxford at all, I do not believe he would have known Paxford well enough to "get" the joke. There were some similarities between Paxford and Puddleglum; one can imagine Lewis telling Hooper that Paxford is like Puddleglum, or Puddleglum like Paxford, and Hooper then inferring Paxford as a source. But the real source of Puddleglum is Lewis's sheer dramatic delight in presenting die-hard pessimism.

Jill, Eustace, and Puddleglum journey north to the land of the giants (in Norse mythology the frost giants who fought the gods lived in the far northern reaches of the Earth) and hear the giants arguing "in long meaningless words of about twenty syllables each" (70). Ideally, Lewis would probably have liked the giants to speak in his books in words befitting their size, but the vocabulary limitations on children's books did not permit that. Clearly, however, he tries to create an impression of the giants liking and using polysyllabic words, both here and in the other Chronicles as well. The giants' names throughout the series are longer than the names of other characters, Rumblebuffin and Wimbleweather being two examples. The shock the children get on seeing the giant king's tongue come out displays similarities to the Brobdingnagian section of *Gulliver's Travels*, where Gulliver repeatedly expresses his disgust at seeing the skin and faces of the gigantic Brobdingnagians up close.

After escaping from the giants, Jill, Eustace, and Puddleglum explore the large "under me" cut in stone, which the Black Knight explains to them is part of an old poem: "Though under Earth and throneless now I be, / Yet, while I lived, all Earth was under me" (133). The knight explains that this boast came from an ancient king who had it cut into stone; now it ironically lies in pieces. The idea matches Percy Shelley's "Ozymandias," in which "Ozymandias, king of kings" has carved into stone the boast, "Look on my works, ye mighty, and despair" (Norton 535). At the time of the poem, the statue over the boast is in fragments.

The words "under me," being connected with the Signs, have an element of Scripture to them, and Lewis uses this section to bring forth some of his adult views regarding the reliability of Scripture. The Black Knight, a "liberal theologian," patronizingly remarks regarding the words, "Is it not the merriest jest in the world that you should have thought they were written to you?" (134). Puddleglum, here speaking for Lewis, responds, "There are no accidents. Our guide is Aslan; and he was there when the giant king caused the letters to be cut, and he knew already all things that would come of them; including this" (134).

This is a fictionalized children's version of Lewis's argument for meaning in Scripture. A clear adult presentation of this can be found in a book written in the same decade as the Chronicles were—*Reflections on the Psalms*. There Lewis argues that Christ expects people to find meaning in the Scriptures and uses a form of Puddleglum's argument that the natural events leading to Scripture formation were part of Aslan's, or God's, overall plan: "Thus something originally merely natural—the kind of myth that is found among most nations—will have been raised by God above itself, qualified by Him and compelled by Him to serve purposes which of itself it would not have served" (*Reflections* 111).

Lewis's views on women appear again in this conversation, as Jill tells the knight, "Where I come from . . . they don't think much of men who are bossed about by their wives" (139). Once again, "they" is a euphemism for Lewis. He felt any right-thinking person would automatically agree with male headship. In an April 18, 1940, letter to a former female student, for instance, he puts his views on marriage headship into a series of rhetorical questions, assuming the "correct" answers are obvious: "Do you really want the Head to be the woman? . . . Do you really like women in authority? When you seek authority yourself, do you naturally seek it in a woman?" (*Letters* 349–50). To Lewis, the answer was clearly no.

The three travelers decide to watch the knight go through his enchantment. He warns them not to release him no matter what words he might use. Lewis uses the clever twist of having the knight during his "pre-chair" (evil) phase reverse phrases from Scripture, so readers who are familiar with the originals will be led to oppose what the knight is saying. For instance, the knight tells the travelers to "harden your hearts and stop your ears" (142). This is a direct reversal of several biblical passages to "harden not your hearts" (e.g., Heb. 3:8; 4:7) and to "give ear" to the words of wisdom (Isa. 28:23; Jer. 13:15, etc.). Since the knight is reversing scriptural advice, biblically literate readers are being encouraged to distrust him at this stage. When the knight during the enchantment scene returns to his real (good) self—though the travelers believe he is now becoming enchanted—Lewis shows this by having him agree with texts of Scripture rather than reversing them. For instance, he accuses the travelers of having "hearts of stone" (144). In the Bible people who make this accusation (as in Zech. 7:12, where the Israelites "made their hearts as an adamant stone") always speak from a righteous point of view, so we are led to believe that the knight is now on the side of right. Finally the travelers come to this conclusion, and in a sort of exorcism scene done "in the name of Aslan," they free the knight, who is actually Prince Rilian (146).

Almost immediately the witch comes in, however, and she engages the travelers and the prince in one of the philosophical dialogues that Lewis likes to insert into his novels, of which the best known is the one that extends over several chapters of *Perelandra*.

And just as Lewis ended that dialogue with a physical action, a fist-fight, he ends this one with Puddleglum stamping out the witch's fire and burning his feet. The "pain itself made Puddleglum's head for a moment perfectly clear. . . . There is nothing like a good shock of pain for dissolving certain kinds of magic" (158). Lewis had, of course, written a famous book on pain in the preceding decade, and this paragraph parallels and supports the most famous line from that book, that pain is "God's megaphone to rouse a deaf world" (*Problem* 93).

The witch's limbs entwine with her body, and she turns into a serpent, coiling around Rilian. He grabs her by the neck and, with Puddleglum's assistance, chops off her head. This image owes a debt to both Milton and Spenser. In *Paradise Lost* 10.512–14, after Satan has caused Adam and Eve to fall and has returned to hell, he gives a boastful speech to the demonic audience. At the end of the speech, however, he suddenly feels himself transforming: "His Arms clung to his Ribs, his Legs entwining / Each other, till supplanted down he fell / a monstrous Serpent on his Belly prone" (Milton 418). The battle itself incorporates elements of the fight between Error and the Red Crosse Knight in *Faerie Queene* 1.1.18–19, 24: Error: "All suddenly about his body wound / . . . Wherewith he grypt her gorge [throat] with so great paine / . . . He raft her hateful head without remorse" (Spenser 10–12).

After the witch is killed, the Underlanders are free to return to their land of Bism, which seems a cross between *abyss* and *chasm*. In response to a question from Rilian, Golg, one of the Underlanders, asserts that they do not actually live in the world's internal fires: "It's only salamanders live in the fire itself" (181). This line of medieval biological folklore comes from Pliny, the Roman naturalist whose erroneous biological statements litter the literature of the Middle Ages. Underland contains a "sunless sea" (185), reminiscent of Samuel Coleridge's phrase in the fourth and fifth lines of his poem "Kubla Khan": "Through caverns measureless to man, / Down to a sunless sea."

Eventually the travelers return to Narnia to find that King Caspian has died. Since Caspian was Aslan's friend, "the Lion wept" (211), and the reader is reminded that at the death of Christ's friend

Lazarus, "Jesus wept" (John 11:35). The two stories converge in their main feature as well, since Christ resurrects Lazarus and Aslan resurrects Caspian. In a different biblical overtone, the thorn driven into Aslan's paw to produce resurrecting blood parallels the spike driven into Christ's hands.

Caspian, Jill, Eustace, and Aslan enter our world to chastise the bullies of Jill's and Eustace's school. The bullies "shall see only my back" (214), Aslan states, perhaps a reference to Exodus 33, where God announces that no one (in our world) can see his face and live, so in response to Moses' request to see him, God shows only his back. Turning toward Jill and Eustace, Aslan "breathed upon them and touched their foreheads with his tongue" (214–15), a clear reference to the strengthening of the Holy Spirit at Pentecost, when the apostle received "tongues like as of fire, and it sat upon each of them" (Acts 2:3b). The breathing assimilates both the biblical wind accompanying the tongues of fire and the traditional association of the Holy Spirit and air movement (since in Greek, *pneuma* means both "wind" and "spirit").

The bullies are whipped with a riding crop and beaten with swords in a scene that has bothered many readers, but which one imagines gave Lewis a sort of vicarious pleasure. He then mentions the "hysterics" of the head of the school "who was, by the way, a woman" (215). That parenthetical phrase lets *Chair* end, as it began, with biography: Lewis's detestation of bullies and women in education.

*Chair* is rarely selected by readers as their favorite Chronicle (in polls of readers *Lion* generally wins while *Chair* and *Caspian* finish at the bottom), and Lewis's allusion choices to some extent explain why. The literary references are generally obscure ones, particularly compared to the biblical references seen so often in the preceding books. More seriously, Lewis's frequent use of biographical references to an unpleasant period of his life sometimes creates an underlying bitterness of tone that may distance some readers, especially some of his antifeminist remarks and the apparent thirst for vengeance of the novel's close. The plot and theme are strong, but the biographical allusions are uncongenial.

# CHAPTER 6

# "Myself": Allusions in *The Horse and His Boy*

*The Horse and His Boy* is one of the least allusive of the Chronicles of Narnia. (*The Last Battle* is also sparse in allusions for reasons I will note when we come to that book.) To some extent this may be because it has the least connection with our world; unlike the other books, this one contains no transposition scene wherein someone from our planet determines to enter or is drawn into Narnia. In only two chapters do people from our world have major speaking roles. Also, *Horse* is a different type of novel from the others in the first half dozen. *Lion* and *Nephew* are retellings of events in our world; *Treader* is a journey novel; *Caspian* and *Chair* are novels of "setting things right," in which people from our world interact with Narnians to overcome evil. Only *Horse* is a novel of the type Lewis liked so much, a rollicking adventure story filled with local color. A final feature that tends to hold down the number of allusions in *Horse* is that being set in the southernmost region of Lewis's mythical world limits the elements of Norse mythology that would normally have sprung to his mind.

The opening of *Horse* is set in Calormen, the Turkish/Arabic/Persian-flavored land that served Lewis as the Narnian equivalent of the Muslim countries of the Middle Ages. "Calormen," as previously noted, stems from the Latin *calor*, meaning "heat," to show it is a hot country. Calormen is literally, then, where men live in the heat. It is certainly no accident that Narnia is located in the North and Calormen in the South. Apart from geographical affinities in our own world, Lewis always associated his deepest emotional longings with what he called "Northerness": "Pure 'Northerness' engulfed me: a vision of huge, clear spaces hanging above the Atlantic in the endless twilight of Northern summer. . . . Northerness seemed then a bigger thing than my religion" (*Surprised* 73, 76). Lewis's longings are portrayed to some extent in Shasta, who "was very interested in everything that lay to the north" and "would often look eagerly to the north" (2).

On a more prosaic level, Lewis physically preferred northern to southern weather. Walter Hooper says Lewis once described himself as having the "constitution of a polar bear" and used to call temperatures near eighty degrees "suffocating," "blistering," and "scorching" (*Past* 74).

The high lords of Narnia are known as "Tarkaans," with the second syllable presumably suggested by the Turkish *khan,* meaning "lord" (as in "Kublai Khan"). The double *a* is an unusual combination in English; Lewis used it to create a sense of "Middle Easterness," since in English (aside from *aardvark* and a few other instances borrowed from Afrikaans) most words with double *a* are names connected with the Middle East. (Hence the title *Kazaam* for the 1996 Shaquille O'Neal cartoon movie.) Familiar biblical examples are Baal, Aaron, and Canaan. It is worth noting, by the way, that while the other six Chronicles are filled with blended names and names with an Anglo-Saxon or Middle English origin, *Horse* has virtually none of these. Since most of the characters are not northern, Lewis can't use northern-sounding origins, and he is apparently not comfortable enough with Middle Eastern languages to combine words into names effectively. Generally in *Horse* his technique is simply to use letter combinations that sound "Middle Eastern," such as the double *a* or the *sh* of *Shasta, Rabadash,* and *Ahoshta* (which we are most familiar with today in the name of Salmon Rushdie and the Middle Eastern movie flop *Ishtar*), or to use a Middle Eastern letter combination with a Middle Eastern syllable, as in *Tarkaan* and *Tashbaan.*

The scene in which Bree the horse teaches Shasta to ride comes from one of Lewis's own desires. As he wrote to his goddaughter Sarah about riding horses: "I can't, but I love the sight and sound and smell and feel of a horse and v[ery] much wish that I could. I'd sooner have a nice, thickset, steady-going cob [gentle horse] that knew me & that I knew how to ride than all the cars and private planes in the world" (*Letters to Children* 37).

Shasta discovers that free Narnians do not use the Calormen (i.e., Middle Eastern) phrase about the Tisroc, "May he live forever." The phrase appears, among other places, in the biblical book of Daniel, where before people begin a speech to the Persian ruler, they preface it by saying, "O King, live for ever" (as in Dan. 6:21). Lewis generally tends to use sources that fit well with the atmosphere he is trying to create, and it is significant that the biblical book of Daniel, unused in the other *Chronicles*, figures occasionally in this novel. *Horse* is set in Calormen rather than Narnia; Daniel is set in Babylonia rather than Israel. Daniel's Oriental underpinnings for a Middle Eastern nation exactly suited Lewis's plan for *Horse*.

Another reminiscent phrase appears in the Aravis-Shasta conversation where he reveals his dismay at her allowing her servant to be whipped. Aravis irritatedly responds, "I did not do any of these things for the sake of pleasing you" (40). Given Lewis's Renaissance background, readers may suspect an echo here of Orlando's response to Jacques in Shakespeare's *As You Like It* 3.2.266, when Jacques declares he does not like Rosalind's name: "There was no thought of pleasing you when she was christened" (Shakespeare 385).

In the same conversation Shasta questions the truth of Aravis's betrothal story, drawing attention to her youth and asking, "How could you be getting married at your age?" Bree, ever the put-down artist, responds, "Shasta, don't display your ignorance. They're always married at that age in the great Tarkaan families" (40). Although Bree's answer is directed toward Shasta, it is secondarily aimed at the reader, who may have been wondering the same thing.

Since *Horse,* like all the Chronicles, has a medieval setting, Lewis uses medieval marriage ages. Bree and Aravis understand early marriage ages while Shasta does not because they have lived among the aristocracy, where the early marriage tradition flourishes. As Frances and Joseph Gies note in their thorough study *Marriage and Family in the Middle Ages,* "Child marriage was confined to the aristocracy, peasant and artisan classes having no need of it" (209). Regarding actual ages, they point out that for the fourteenth century, "women married as early as fourteen" (185). As most readers will recall, both Juliet Capulet and her upper-class mother married (or in the case of her mother, gave birth) at the age of thirteen, a fact that caused no confusion for Elizabethan audiences.

Hwin, Bree, Shasta, and Aravis make their way to Calormen's capital, Tashbaan, named after the Calormen god, Tash. The name *Tash* may owe something to the Middle Eastern city Tashkent; *ban* is a seventeenth-century Persian word meaning "lord." Thus *Tashbaan* (with the *a* doubled for Middle Eastern effect) is the city where Tash is lord. In the city our focus changes temporarily to Edmund and Susan Pevensie, who are also discussing marriage plans. When Susan suggests leaving, Edmund responds, "There's the rub" (62). It is hard to imagine any educated adult reader not recognizing the phrase from Hamlet's "To be or not to be" speech. This is an instance of something fairly rare in the Chronicles, a case where a reader who does not recognize the allusion will probably not understand the meaning of the sentence.

The meeting in the Narnian guesthouse of look-alikes Shasta and Corin is an obvious parallel of Mark Twain's *The Prince and the Pauper,* with Corin as the prince and Shasta as the pauper. Lewis was an enthusiastic reader of Twain, though he thought after *Tom Sawyer* and (especially) *Huckleberry Finn,* there was a great falling-off in the quality of Twain's work.

The plot returns to Aravis, who with Lasaraleen is trapped in the room where Prince Rabadash, Ahoshta, and the Tisroc have their conference. Lewis mentions the turban and scimitar of Rabadash to create an Arabic flavor. He also mentions a piece of furniture in the room, in perhaps the most subtle and admirable piece of linguistic wordplay yet found in the Chronicles. When Aravis and Lasaraleen enter the room on page 102, they notice a sofa, which they later have to hide behind. It continues to be a sofa on pages 103 and 104, in three other mentions. Then when the Tisroc, Rabadash, and Ahoshta enter at the bottom of page 104, Lewis begins calling the sofa a "divan," and he continues labeling it a divan through the next chapter until all the Calormene men have left. Why?

First, let us consider some of the main linguistic choices possible for this piece of furniture: couch, davenport, settee, settle, sofa, divan. *Couch* comes from Old French through Middle English; *davenport* comes from the (British) maker's name; *settee* and *settle* come from Anglo-Saxon through Middle English; *sofa* and *divan* come from Turkish. Lewis avoids, then, the four choices deriving from a British background and uses only the two with a Middle Eastern origin. That sort of linguistic sophistication in itself sets him apart from virtually every other novelist.

But there is a subtle linguistic difference between the two choices. While *sofa* merely means a piece of furniture, *divan* has three main meanings in Turkish (and, by derivation, in English). One is, of course, the article of furniture. Another meaning, a collection of poetry by a single author with a complicated alphabetic rhyme scheme, does not come into play here (although as a literary term Lewis would surely have known it). The final signification of the word is, as the *Oxford English Dictionary* puts it, "an Oriental council of state." Another dictionary gave the meaning, "a private political conference, particularly in Renaissance-era Turkey." And of course a private political conference is exactly what we have here when Rabadash, Ahoshta, and the Tisroc enter the room.

Thus, when there is no council going on, Lewis repeatedly and exclusively uses the word *sofa*, with no political overtones; and from the moment the council members enter, he repeatedly and exclusively switches to the word with political connotations, *divan*. This cannot be mere chance. When *divan* entered the English language in 1586, according to the *Oxford English Dictionary,* its original meaning was the political one, making it even more likely that Lewis would have come across that connotation in the literature of the period. One place he would certainly have met the word is in *Paradise Lost* 10.456–70, where Milton describes the reaction of the leading demons to the triumphant return of Satan after the fall of humanity: "Forth rush'd in haste the great consulting Peers, / Rais'd from their dark Divan" (Milton 417). The gathered demons are not all sitting on the same couch; Milton is using the word in the "council of state" sense. Thus so small a thing as the label for a piece of furniture reveals Lewis's love of antique words and his linguistic subtlety. One cannot help but suspect that there are similar linguistic veins of ore hidden throughout the Chronicles; probably the patience of etymological scholars will enable us to mine more deeply in the twenty-first century and foster greater admiration for this aspect of Lewis's writing.

When Aravis is able to get away from the divan (in both senses), she meets with Shasta, Bree, and Hwin on the far side of Tashbaan. They hear about the plan of Rabadash to secretly invade Archenland, and as usual Bree produces the strongest reaction: "We'll grease his oats for him" (122). One of Lewis's cleverer features is his ability to let talking animals retain the interests of animals, even into their proverbial sayings. A good example occurs in the fifth chapter of *Horse,* where Sallowpad the Raven realizes that the Narnians need to make plans. Rather than phrasing this the traditional human way ("A stitch in time saves nine"), he uses a traditional bird equivalent, "nests before eggs" (70). Bree's saying is intended to say something negative about Rabadash, but what?

An answer can be found in *King Lear* 2.4.123–24. A character comments that a man who does a harmful thing with good intentions is like a man who, "in pure kindness to his horse, buttered his hay." Buttered hay is clearly similar to greased oats. David Bevington, in his commentary on the line, notes that "horses do not like greasy hay" (1190). So by greasing Rabadash's oats, Bree is saying that their band will do something unpalatable, something Rabadash won't like.

61

Eventually Shasta, Aravis, and the horses reach the Hermit of the Southern March. *Hermit* often has religious connotations, and in this case the hermit is a sort of mystical religious figure. Lewis connects him with Francis of Assisi by having him refer to the horses and goats as "cousins." Shasta leaves the hermit to encounter King Lune of Archenland. I am not aware of any maps Lewis drew to show the exact borders he had in mind for Archenland, but he appears to have pictured it roughly in the shape of an arch. The country's name is not alone sufficient evidence for that supposition, but the ruler's name is King Lune, and *lune* entered the language around 1700 in the meaning of "an arch or crescent shape"; thus the names of the country and its ruler form a linguistic pair.

Finally Shasta meets Aslan and asks why he wounded Aravis, to which he gets the reply, "I tell no-one any story but his own" (159), a principle later broken in *Nephew*. Shasta then asks who Aslan is and hears: "'Myself,' said the Voice, very deep and low so that the earth shook: and again 'Myself' loud and clear and gay: and then the third time 'Myself,' whispered so softly you could hardly hear it, and yet it seemed to come from all round you as if the leaves rustled with it" (159).

The pronoun comes from the sacred Hebrew name for God, the tetragrammaton, YHWH, usually Anglicized as *Yahweh* or *Jehovah,* and translated as "I am." The relevant biblical passage occurs in Exodus 3, where Moses, like Shasta, asks God his name, and is told, "I am that I am" (Exod. 3:14a). The threefold repetition of "Myself" represents the Trinity, with the deep voice being the Father (for power), the clear voice the Son (for brightness), and the whispered voice the Spirit (for the associations of Greek *pneuma* and Latin *spiritus* with breath and wind that have been earlier discussed). This matching of different words with appropriate members of the Trinity occurs occasionally in English Renaissance religious poetry. The most famous example would be John Donne's "Batter My Heart, Three-Personed God," where he asks God the Father to "knock," God the Son to "shine," and God the Spirit to "breathe."

As Shasta gazes at Aslan, and then at the spot Aslan had left, Lewis fills the paragraphs with traditional religious imagery, most of which has been noted in earlier sections. Light streams from Aslan; he touches his tongue to Shasta's forehead. After Aslan leaves, the ground where his front paw (appropriately, the *right* paw) has rested fills with water—living water, since it overflows and creates a stream. Shasta drinks from this living water and is refreshed.

He then meets with Corin, who tells him eagles are circling because they can tell battle is imminent; "They know we're preparing a feed for them" is the way Corin puts it (176). The choice of eagles here rather than vultures or buzzards seems strange to many contemporary readers. Lewis's sources are the Bible and Anglo-Saxon literature; both the Old and New Testaments refer to eagles as eaters of carrion. One example is Matthew 24:28: "For wheresoever the carcase [carcass] is, there will the eagles be gathered together." The idea that birds could sense forthcoming battle is a standard one in Anglo-Saxon writing. One of Lewis's favorite poems from that period, "The Battle of Maldon," contains the lines: "The time had come when doomed men should fall. Shouts were raised; raven circled, the eagle eager for food" (Abrams 91).

When the battle ends, Shasta reveals to Aravis that he is actually Prince Cor (a form of the French *coeur,* or *heart,* since Shasta has shown such a stout heart throughout the novel). Shasta says he's pleased even "though Education and all sorts of horrible things are going to happen to me" (197), an obvious reference to Lewis's own painful educational experience as detailed in *Chair.* Shasta tells how at his birth he was kidnapped by the Lord Chancellor, Lord Bar, *bar* being the sixteenth-century collective term for attorneys, still in use today in the phrase "admitted to the bar." The Lord Chancellor had been discovered embezzling and had been removed from office but otherwise went unpunished. This parallels English Renaissance history; in a famous episode from the time of King James I the Lord Chancellor of England, Lord Francis Bacon, had also been caught embezzling and had equally been removed from office but gone otherwise unpunished.

With Shasta thus accounted for, the novel's denouement wraps up the loose ends of Bree and Rabadash. Bree decides to enter Narnia, but with great reluctance; Lewis says "he looked more like a horse going to a funeral than a long-lost captive going to home and freedom" (202). This entry into Narnia sounds deliberately fashioned after Lewis's description of his own entry into Christianity: "I gave in, and admitted God was God, and knelt and prayed: perhaps, that night, the most dejected and reluctant convert in all England" (*Surprised* 228–29).

Prince Rabadash is indeed a dashing figure in most of the novel; and for Lewis *dash* is a pejorative term, particularly for rulers. In "De Descriptione Temporum," his inaugural lecture at Cambridge University, Lewis noted that one of the flaws of the modern world was its desire for "dash" in its leaders rather than the older virtues of diligence and incorruption.

After Rabadash is captured, he hurls curses upon the Narnians and Archenlanders, but King Lune urges them not to be "chafed by the taunt of a pajock" (207). This, like the use of *uglification* in *Treader,* is a rare case where Lewis's literary source for a single word can almost certainly be pinned down, for the usual Renaissance spelling for this now obsolete word is *paiocke,* but the spelling in *Hamlet* 3.2.284, from which Lewis almost certainly took the word, is *pajock.* No one today knows the exact meaning of the word. Even if the unusual spelling were not enough to certify *Hamlet* as the source, context clues provide further support. In the use of the word in *Hamlet,* Hamlet is making fun of Claudius to Horatio by creating a piece of light verse: "'For thou dost know, O Damon dear, / This realm dismantled was / Of Jove himself, and now reigns here / A very, very—pajock." To this Horatio smartly replies, "You might have rhymed" (Shakespeare 1165). Since *was* was pronounced in Renaissance London to rhyme with *pass,* obviously the rhyming word Hamlet has omitted from Claudius's description is *ass.* Significantly, Lewis's use of *pajock* for Rabadash comes at the point where Rabadash is about to be turned into an ass. Rabadash, in fact, is called an ass on page 211.

The turning of Rabadash into an ass is in some ways another borrowing from the book of Daniel. In the fourth chapter the Babylonian ruler Nebuchadnezzar made a speech filled with pride, akin to the one made by Rabadash. A "voice from heaven" (like the voice of Aslan in *Horse*) announced that Nebuchadnezzar would become as a beast, losing his reason; "and he was driven from men, and did eat grass as oxen, and his body was wet with the dew of heaven" (Dan. 4:33b). Although the biblical text does not specify an animal body for Nebuchadnezzar, many readers have inferred the form of an ass. Eventually, as with Rabadash, Nebuchadnezzar regained both his humanity and his royal power.

It will be noted that the commentary on *Horse* reveals fewer allusions than the previous works contain; I have given some reasons for this at the opening of the chapter. But particularly striking in *Horse* is the almost complete absence of mythology, and this merits a closing comment. The absence of Norse mythology is easy to explain; Norse myth is associated with the North, and *Horse* is set in the South. But even with a Calormene setting, *Horse* could have elements of Greek and Roman myths, since those are set in warm climates. And certainly it seems *Horse* should, being set in a hot and dry climate, have elements of Arabian mythology. Why, one might ask, are there no references to genies and lamps and Sinbads and "open sesames" in this novel?

An immediate and to some extent satisfactory answer is that Lewis simply didn't know Arabian mythology as well as he knew the Greek and Norse. It is true that, having read less in that field, he had fewer elements spring unbidden to his mind. But as I noted in the chapter on *Lion*, Lewis probably read a good bit of Arabic literature during the 1940s while working on the Manzalaoui Arabic/English translation thesis. So he did have some acquaintance with Arabian stories, and in fact elements from them come into play in other novels of the series. In *Lion*, for instance, the name of Aslan comes from Lane's *Arabian Nights*, as noted earlier. And in the same book

Mr. Beaver tells the Pevensies that the witch is descended from the Jinn, which are figures from Arabian demonology with the power to assume alternate shapes, a power given to the witch as well. So Lewis was neither unacquainted with Arabian mythology nor unwilling to use it. Why, then, is mythology virtually absent from *Horse*?

One of Lewis's key beliefs was that virtually all mythologies have elements of truth and to some extent can lift people toward the "true myth" of Christianity. This view was of overwhelming importance for Lewis because this was the point that in September 1931 led to his becoming a Christian. His close friends Hugo Dyson and J. R. R. Tolkien, in a conversation after dinner that lasted till 3:00 a.m., reminded Lewis of how moving and valuable he found myth to be in general. In reflecting upon this, Lewis came to believe that "the story of Christ is simply a true myth: a myth working on us in the same way as the others, but with this tremendous difference that *it really happened*. . . . The Pagan stories are God expressing Himself through the minds of poets, using such images as He found there, while Christianity is God expressing Himself through what we call 'real things'" (Green and Hooper 118, emphasis Lewis's).

So for Lewis it could almost be said that mythology is an element of religious revelation. It is seeing through a glass darkly but still seeing. Calormen has, or should have, a sort of mythology associated with the god Tash; but except for Emeth in *Battle,* the Calormenes do not really seem to believe in Tash or any stories connected with him. The Calormenes in *Horse* are, as Lewis would pejoratively say, very practical, and mythology does not appear to have much to do with the practical world.

What sort of literature is "practical"? Proverbs are, and thus the Calormene political leaders repeatedly speak in proverbs, with the Tisroc, the chief leader, being the most proverbial of all. It is noteworthy that, although there is a book of Proverbs in the Bible, Lewis did not find it spiritually nourishing. In his voluminous writings I am aware of only two occasions where he quoted from the book of Proverbs, although he did cite with some frequency from the other

Old Testament books of poetry (Job, Psalms, Ecclesiastes, Song of Solomon). One instance where Lewis quotes from Proverbs indicates clearly his feelings regarding the book. In writing upon the Psalms, Lewis notes that Proverbs 25:21 ("If thine enemy be hungry, give him bread to eat, and if he be thirsty, give him water to drink") comes as a surprisingly enlightened concept. Why did Lewis find it so startling that there would be something really good in Proverbs? His view of the book as a whole explains why: "What a dull, remote thing, for example, the Book of Proverbs seems at a first glance: bearded Orientals uttering endless platitudes as if in a parody of the *Arabian Nights*. Compared with Plato or Aristotle—or even with Xenophon—it is not *thought* at all" (*Reflections* 115, emphasis his).

Significantly, Lewis finds the book of Proverbs to sound "Arabian," a term of disdain in the context of the Chronicles. The difference between the proverbs of Calormen and the mythological elements of Narnia is Lewis's way of illustrating that (in his view) a country nourished on mythology will be religiously healthier than a country nourished on practical proverbs.

# CHAPTER 7

# "The Founding of Narnia": Allusions in *The Magician's Nephew*

*The Magician's Nephew* begins with the pretense that fictional works have reality; Lewis says the story takes place in the days when "Mr. Sherlock Holmes was still living in Baker Street and the Bastables were looking for treasure in the Lewisham Road" (1). As was noted in *Caspian,* Lewis was a Holmes fan; in fact, while he was growing up, his family subscribed to *Strand,* the magazine where the stories were first published, before they appeared in book form. Presumably he read some of the stories in their original setting. The Bastables are the children in the works of Edith Nesbitt, such as *Three Children and It,* which Lewis loved as both a child and an adult.

In some ways *Nephew* is the most-autobiographical of the Chronicles, since one of the two main human characters, Digory Kirke, has several fairly close parallels to Lewis. Digory has a "funny name" (like Clive Staples!) and a dying mother; he lives in the first decade of the twentieth century; he wishes he had a pony; he grows up to be a professor who takes in children during World War II. Digory misses his father, who is in India, and it may not be too fanciful in this regard to remember how Lewis missed his army-officer brother Warnie, serving in India. In addition, just two weeks after the death of his mother, Lewis was sent to England to school, while his father stayed in Ireland; thus the two of them were separated for most of Lewis's later childhood.

Digory Kirke and Polly Plummer, the other main character, are both readers, as is evidenced by the fact that Digory tosses into their conversation a casual reference to *Treasure Island* and Polly seems familiar with the book. As I noted in chapter 3, Lewis had difficulty imagining children who had not read through all the classic juvenile works by age ten. Lewis himself had read *Paradise Lost* by age nine, so even a less precocious child, he seemed to feel, would have read all the standard works for children by ten or eleven. There is some question, it should be said, about the age of Polly. In the "Outline of Narnian History" that Walter Hooper said he received from Lewis, Polly's age in *Nephew* is given as eleven. This seems fairly accurate to me (I would estimate her at 10–11) and thus makes problematic the line when Polly first sees the rings. According to Lewis, had she "been a very little younger she would have wanted to put one in her mouth" (10). Why would a ten-year-old girl want to suck on a piece of jewelry? Lewis would never have made so odd a statement about a boy; it's an example of his curious and long-held belief that girls mature more slowly than boys.

Since the summer days are rainy, as Lewis remembered from his youth, Digory and Polly go exploring. They try to figure out mathematically how far they need to explore through the back way to get to an empty house. Lewis says, "When they had measured the attic they had to get a pencil and do a sum. They both got different answers to it at first, and even when they agreed I am not sure they got it right" (8). Actually, they did not get it right, since they ended up in the wrong house! Many writers create fictional characters in their own image, and Lewis more than most; the picture of two literate but innumerate children is an exact replica of the young Lewis (and the older Lewis, for that matter). When Lewis took (and failed) the math exam to enter Oxford, for instance, he was, to use his own phrase, "handsomely plowed."

Polly and Digory enter Uncle Andre's study, where he tells them about his godmother, Mrs. LeFay. This is, of course, the evil witch

Morgan LeFay of Arthurian legend. LeFay gave Andrew a box from Atlantis before her death, which Andrew said he could tell was a significant box "by the pricking in my fingers" (17–18). Renaissance folklore presented witches and magicians as having tingling sensations in their fingers when near something especially evil or powerful; Lewis would have been familiar with this concept from various sources, notably *Macbeth* 4.1.44–45, wherein the second witch says as Macbeth draws near, "By the pricking of my thumbs, / Something wicked this way comes" (Shakespeare 1329).

Lewis clarifies for us that Andrew is an evil character by the way he mistreats guinea pigs. Lewis was an animal lover his whole life, who had pet mice as a child and pet dogs and cats as an adult. One sign of the Unman's evil in *Perelandra*, as Lewis presents him, is that he tortures frogs. An entire chapter of *The Problem of Pain* is given to the problem of animal pain, making it all the odder that Madeleine L'Engle, in her foreword to Paul Ford's *Companion to Narnia*, should accuse Lewis of "a total lack of sensitivity toward the pain of animals. It would seem that to him it did not matter whether or not animals were hurt—his most unEnglish trait!" (xiv). It would indeed be an un-English trait if Lewis possessed it, but he did not; the fact that Digory reacts with anger to the deaths of the guinea pigs instructs us in how we are to respond.

Using their magic rings, Polly and Digory come to the land of Charn, where they meet Jadis. Except for her, all the people of Charn are dead, killed by her magic use of the "Deplorable Word." *Charn* may be a cross of *charm,* from her magic, and *charnel,* a charnel house being an abode for the dead. The Deplorable Word Jadis uses to destroy the world refers to the atomic bomb, which had been used in war for the first time only about eight years before this book was written. The Deplorable Word ended the three-day battle over Charn, which perhaps owes something to the three-day battle over heaven in *Paradise Lost.*

When Jadis arrives in our world, Andrew discovers that the power he wanted has come, but instead of him controlling it, it controls him; Jadis calls him her slave. This illustrates a point from

Lewis's adult nonfiction book *The Abolition of Man*: "It is the magician's bargain: give up our soul, get power in return. But once our souls, that is, our selves, have been given up, the power thus conferred will not belong to us. We shall in fact be the slaves and puppets of that to which we have given our souls" (Lewis 83–84).

This is another example of Lewis's attempts to bring the moral or spiritual insights from his adult nonfiction into his children's fiction. In the adult book the point is that humans can become enslaved to a lust for power; in the children's book this is shown literally. The spiritual force stronger than ourselves becomes a tangible being stronger than ourselves.

This same power twist can be seen in the opening act of one of the most famous Renaissance tragedies, Christopher Marlowe's *Dr. Faustus*. Like Uncle Andrew, Dr. Faustus conjures, and he is delighted to find that he "made" the demon Mephistophilis appear. But Mephistophilis tells Faustus, "No, I came now hither of mine own accord" (Abrams 998). When Faustus tries to argue that he made Mephistophilis appear, Mephistophilis says he came simply because he thought he could take away Faustus's soul.

When Jadis tries to dominate our world, Digory attempts to remove her by grabbing her heel while he holds the magic ring. She kicks him in the mouth, but he is eventually able to use her heel to pull her away. While one might see a reference to Achilles's heel here, more likely Lewis is referring to Genesis, in which enmity is put between humanity and the serpent, with God declaring to the serpent that humanity "shall bruise thy head, and thou shalt bruise his heel" (Gen. 3:15a). This imagery had already been used by Lewis a decade earlier in *Perelandra* where the righteous Ransom crushes the head of the evil Unman while receiving a wound to the heel.

When Polly, Digory, Andrew, Jadis, and Frank (the cabby) arrive in Narnia, they are cowed by the dark emptiness of the as yet uncreated world, and the cabby suggests singing a hymn with a line about crops "safely gathered in" (97). This is "Come, Ye Thankful People Come," written by Henry Alford in 1844; the phrase mentioned is in the third line of the first verse. Singing is a running motif of this creation saga. Aslan sings Narnia into being, echoing sources that say the universe began with song. Lewis would have been familiar, for instance, with the opening lines of Dryden's "A Song for St. Cecilia's Day, 1687": "From harmony, from heav'nly harmony / This universal frame began" (Dryden 73). In response to Aslan's song, the five visitors can hear the stars singing, the Renaissance concept called "the music of the spheres." This description owes a debt to the biblical account of how when our world was created "the morning stars sang together" (Job 38:7a).

After Aslan has created the animals, he selects some of them two at a time to be his followers. The selecting of animals by twos naturally reminds one of Noah's ark, but perhaps more useful here is the concept of Israel as God's chosen nation, alluded to by describing the selected animals as "chosen beasts" who "followed him [Aslan]" (115). Aslan warns the talking animals that they can, if disobedient, revert to dumb beasts, "for out of them you were taken and into them you can return" (118), a clear allusion to Genesis 3:19b, in which God says to Adam (literally "man"), "out of it [dust] wast thou taken: for dust thou art, and unto dust shalt thou return."

Aslan announces to the chosen beasts that "an evil" has entered the world. He leaves with a select council, and the other animals in discussing the situation remark, "What did he say had entered the world? A Neevil" (119). Lewis playfully presents this as a Narnian instance of a linguistic phenomenon he was familiar with from English, the moving of a letter from the end of one word to the start of another (or vice versa). This most commonly occurs with the letter *n*. For instance, the old English word for snake was *a naedre*, which now has turned into "an adder," because people heard the word differently. An example going the opposite way is "a newt," originally *an ewt*. Another item from this chapter of linguistic interest is the now archaic word *tantivy*, which the animals use to spur one another on in their chase of Andrew. It means "gallop" and first entered the written language, according to the *Oxford English Dictionary*, in 1641.

In this same chapter the jackdaw (old-fashioned word for crow) misspeaks and, when everyone laughs, the daw asks Aslan, "Have I made the first joke?" To this Aslan replies, "You have not made the first joke; you have only been the first joke." Lewis comments that in response to this "the Jackdaw didn't mind and laughed just as loud" (119). Given the paradisal, virtually unfallen setting, this episode may be reminiscent of an episode in Dante's *Paradiso,* the medieval religious epic. Upon entering heaven, Pope Gregory discovered that he had been mistaken on a point of theology. Lewis told a friend that he approved of Gregory's response: "But hardly had he wakened in this heaven / Than he was moved to laugh at his own delusions" (Dante 312).

Aslan gives the chosen animals further warning about the evil that is to come into the land and adds, "As Adam's race has done the harm, Adam's race shall help to heal it" (136). This alludes to the biblical concept of "the two Adams" which figures prominently in seventeenth-century poetry—the idea that as a human being brought death into the world, so it would take a human being (in our world, Christ in human form) to redeem it. Aslan then takes Digory aside to share their griefs together and comments, "Grief is great. . . . Let us be good to one another" (142). The last sentence is, with only one word altered, exactly taken from one of the great poems on grief from the Victorian era, Matthew Arnold's "Dover Beach": "let us be true to one another" (1356). Aslan's repetition of "My son, my son" uses the traditional Hebrew expression of grief by repetition: familiar biblical examples are Christ's use of "my God, my God" on the cross (Mark 15:34) and David's use of "my son, my son" over the death of Absalom (2 Sam. 18:33).

Aslan then tells Digory to look toward the west for the direction of the paradisical garden. This at first seems odd, since for European Christians the garden of Eden was always located in the East. But as usual Lewis is blending together a variety of sources: this garden in *Nephew* borrows elements from the Bible (garden of Eden), Greek mythology (garden of the Hesperides), Norse mythology (both the garden of Idun and the tree Yggdrasill), and *Paradise Lost* (Milton's description of Eden). In this case Lewis is using the Greek myth of the garden of the Hesperides, sometimes called the Western Garden, which was traditionally located west of Europe.

The garden, Aslan tells Digory, has an apple tree in the center of it. The Greek and Norse sources specify apples as their fruits; the biblical source never specifies, but tradition has for centuries pictured Adam and Eve with apples. Doubtless many readers have been perplexed by the fact that the apples in *Nephew* are "silver" apples, especially since not only is "golden" a more natural word to use for apples anyway, but all of Lewis's source apples, such as those of Idun or in the Hesperides, are specified as golden. In addition, these are apples of great virtue, and using silver rather than gold seems to lessen their status. It is certainly unlike Lewis to go against every tradition, so the perceptive reader must feel there is some logical reason for the change. Indeed there is, but for clarity I need to delay the discussion. A similar apple tree appears in the sixteenth chapter of *Battle,* and in discussing that tree and comparing it with this one, I will show why Lewis chose the coloring he did.

The central position of the tree (which in *Nephew* combines the properties of the biblical trees of Life and of the Knowledge of Good and Evil) may owe something to the tradition that Yggdrasill, the Norse tree of life, occupied the exact center of the earth; but as Ellis Davidson points out, Christian tradition enters in here as well: "The image of the tree that occupied the centre of the world did not wholly die out. It was replaced by the conception of the Christian cross, believed to stand at the midpoint of the earth when it was raised at Calvary, at the spot once occupied by the fatal tree of Eden" (196).

Digory and Polly's transportation to the garden is the flying horse Fledge, with obvious borrowing from Pegasus, the winged horse of Greek mythology. *Fledge* means "to grow the plumage necessary for flight"; its most common use in contemporary English is in the phrase *full-fledged,* meaning "complete." Aslan warns Fledge, "Do not fly too high" (146) in reference to another Greek myth, the story of Icarus. The story is a familiar one to students of Latin, as

Ovid told it in both *Metamorphoses* and *Ars Amatoria.* Icarus and his father Daedalus were prisoners of King Minos of Crete. To escape, Daedalus constructed wings for each of them out of wax and feathers. As they prepared to take off into flight, Daedalus warned Icarus not to fly too near the sun or the wax on their wings would melt. Icarus, excited to find himself flying, soared too high. The wax melted from his wings, and he plunged into the sea. The warning would seem unnecessary in *Nephew,* since Fledge's wings have no wax, but Lewis never omits an opportunity to plant reminders of his favorite stories.

When Digory and Polly arrive at the garden, they discover it to be set on a hill, with a wall all around it, trees growing higher than the wall, and one set of gates facing due east. This description seems modeled after Milton's picture of Eden in *Paradise Lost*; in 4.144–47 and 178–82 he gives all these details. When Digory enters the garden, he finds a "fountain which rose near the middle" (158), again a borrowing from *Paradise Lost*; Milton indicates in 9.73 that part of the Tigris River, having gone underground, "rose up like a fountain by the Tree of Life" (380).

It is notable that when Digory picks the apple for Aslan, "he couldn't help looking at it and smelling it before he put it away" (158), and that makes him decide that the warning about eating the apples "might have been only a piece of advice—and who cares about advice?" (158–59). The flippancy of the "who cares" remark, combined with the earlier episode in the hall of Charn, shows that Digory really understands he is not to eat the apples, but pride makes him want to follow his own inclinations anyway. The specification of "looking at it" plus "smelling it," combined with "who cares," presents the traditional three-part division of sin used in various literary works of the seventeenth century. The biblical source for this arrangement is 1 John 2:16: "For all that is in the world, the lust of the flesh, and the lust of the eyes, and the pride of life, is not of the Father, but is of the world." Among the seventeenth-century poems using this pattern as an organizing principle is Henry Vaughan's "The World," in which the first stanza describes the lust of the flesh, the second describes the pride of life, the third describes the lust of the eyes, and the fourth says that none of the people committed to these enter heaven. In case we may have missed the biblical connection, Vaughan appends 1 John 2:16 to the end of the poem.

But the three-part concept isn't just a Renaissance or even a New Testament idea; the germ of it can be found in Genesis 3:6a: "And when the woman saw that the tree was good for food, and that is was pleasant to the eyes, and a tree to be desired to make one wise, she took of the fruit thereof, and did eat." This is developed more fully, as one might expect, in *Paradise Lost,* where Milton shows that Eve's original sin encompasses all of the three aspects detailed in 1 John 2:16. When Eve first considers eating the apple in 9.777–78, the three aspects of sin are presented in fairly mild terms; the fruit is "Fair to the Eye, inviting to the Taste, / Of virtue to make one wise" (396). Here we clearly have, in consecutive phrases, the lust of the eye, the lust of the flesh, and the pride of life. When Eve decides to eat the fruit in 9.786 and 790, the three aspects are presented more strongly: "Intent now wholly on her taste [lust of the flesh], naught else / Regarded [lust of the eyes] . . . nor was Godhead from her thought [pride of life]." In the next line Eve eats the apple, so at the last moment Milton reminds us how all of sin was contained in this one act. Similarly Lewis has Digory look at the apple (eyes), smell it (flesh), and argue that he can disregard what anyone says (pride).

At that reflective moment, however, one of the odder aspects of the novel occurs. Lewis, speaking of Digory, says: "While he was thinking of all this he happened to look up through the branches towards the top of the tree. There, on a branch above his head, a wonderful bird was roosting. . . . It was larger than an eagle, its breast saffron, its head crested with scarlet, and its tail purple" (159).

I imagine not a few readers, making connections between Aslan's garden and the garden of Eden, have suddenly been brought up short by this bird in the tree. This is a clear example of the Lewisian style that so annoyed Tolkien, the impulsive mixing of disparate elements. This bird near the top of the tree is the eagle of Yggdrasill from Norse mythology. Lewis specifically compares it to an eagle, making the allusion clearer.

Yggdrasill is the World Tree, the Tree of Life in Norse mythology. A variety of animals clustered near the tree, but the two key ones were the eagle near the top of the tree, representing heaven and the farsighted gods, and the serpent Nithogg (literally, "striker-that-destroys") at the bottom of the tree, representing destruction. The *Prose Edda* describes the situation this way: "In the branches of the ash sits an eagle, and it is very knowledgeable. . . . Words of abuse [are] exchanged between the eagle and Nithogg" (Sturluson 45). The Yggdrasill eagle was famous for its knowledge of what was going on, so it is appropriate that the eaglelike bird in the *Nephew* tree keeps an eye on Digory as he decides whether to eat from the apple.

In studying this Norse account, Lewis would naturally have been reminded of the biblical serpent in Eden and of the eagle associated with Zeus in Greek mythology, a further connection of the eagle with heavenly things. The eagle receives additional symbolism from its coloring; scarlet and purple, as noted earlier, are the ancient colors of royalty. Thus one short paragraph is informed by the Bible, Greek myth, Norse myth, and Roman tradition.

The witch has also entered the garden; she eats from the fruit, then vaults over the wall after Digory. The idea of the evil character eating the tree's fruit parallels *Paradise Lost,* where Eve in her dream at 5.65 watches as Satan "pluckt, he tasted" of the tree. At first Digory thinks the witch must have climbed over the wall, but her quickness leads him to believe she vaulted over it. This fits the description in *Paradise Lost* 4.181–83 of how Satan entered the garden of Eden: "Due entrance he disdain'd, and in contempt, / At one slight bound high overleap'd all bound / Of Hill or highest Wall."

The witch tells Digory that if he doesn't eat an apple he will "miss some knowledge," echoing the biblical description of the tree's virtue. She says it is "the apple of youth, the apple of life. . . . I shall never grow old or die" (161). The life and death imagery clearly stems from the Tree of Life in the biblical account. The "apple of youth" addition may owe an indirect debt to the Greek myth of Tithonus. Tithonus, a mortal, loved Aurora, goddess of the dawn, so he asked for eternal life. His request was granted. Unfortunately, however, Tithonus forgot to request eternal youth, and so he had the wretched outcome of perpetually becoming feebler and more wrinkled. To anyone familiar with that myth, the promise of endless life can be a fearful thing; so by adding youth, Lewis sidetracks a potential reader distraction. Even without the Greek myth, Lewis had sufficient source warrant from Norse mythology for making them apples of youth. Bragi was the Norse god of poetry; his wife, Idun, "guarded the apples of immortality which kept the gods forever young" (Davidson 165). The apples of the Hesperides in Greek myth carried the same power. In addition to youth and immortality, Jadis tells Digory the apples have power to heal, a fact later confirmed by Aslan. This element comes from the apples of Idun in Norse myth.

When Digory finally returns to Aslan with the apple, he is greeted with the approving phrase, "well done" (166). The word choice here echoes the complimentary remark from the biblical parable of the talents in Matthew 25:21a: "Well done, thou good and faithful servant." Aslan and Digory then proceed to the crowning of the first king and queen of Narnia, King Frank and Queen Helen, the cabby and his wife. The names of these two characters are certainly ordinary enough and may be simply chosen at random. Yet, if I may be fanciful for a moment, their names do contain an interesting coincidence. To anyone grounded in Western literary tradition, the name *Helen* automatically suggests Helen of Troy, who was abducted by Paris. And Paris (the city) was in medieval times the capital of the Franks. Helen of Troy and Paris of the Franks? Queen Helen and King Frank? My own feeling is that it's too strained, one of those fanciful interpretations that leads some critics to feel anyone can find wordplay anywhere, but it seemed worth laying before you for a second opinion. After all, Lewis was not above a strained pun. Once a Portuguese dignitary eating haggis (a Scottish food) at an Oxford banquet said he felt like a "gastronomic Columbus." Lewis said a better comparison would be a "vascular da Gama" (Green and

Hooper 125). In case you have forgotten your fifteenth-century world history, Vasco da Gama was the Portuguese explorer who in 1497–98 was able to sail from Portugal around the Cape of Good Hope to India, thereby discovering an all-water route to the Far East. He is, therefore, the Portuguese equivalent of Columbus.

In trying to decide how to best help Andrew, Aslan considers him emblematic of the race and says, "Oh Adam's sons, how cleverly you defend yourselves against all that might do you good!" (171). This line echoes snippets of Christ's similar lament: "O Jerusalem, Jerusalem . . . how often would I have gathered thy children together, even as a hen gathereth her chickens under her wings, and ye would not!" (Matt. 23:37).

In the next section of the novel occurs a situation that, while not specifically allusive, has generated comment and has implications for studying Lewis's use of sources. In the books written before *Nephew,* Lewis set up two key principles of Narnia: that Aslan does not tell people anyone else's story, and that Aslan never tells people what would have happened (had a different choice been made). On pages 174–75 of *Nephew,* these rules are flagrantly broken; it is uncertain whether Lewis simply forgot the rules he had set up or whether he chose to ignore them because they got in the way of the moral points he wanted to make.

Either could have been the case, for Lewis's remarkable memory for the works of others did not extend to his own writings, and he was willing to break his own rules when he felt it necessary. As an example of the former, a young lady wrote to him in August 1953 objecting to his use of the word *kids* in *Prince Caspian.* Lewis defended himself by saying the word was only used once, in a particularly negative way. Then, in a September 19, 1953, letter, Lewis wrote to the young lady again and apologized, saying he had just reread the book and found other instances of his using the word (*Letters to Children* 34).

As for self-contradictions Lewis in a letter gave a young lady this writing advice: "Never exaggerate. Never say more than you really mean" (*Letters to Children* 87). Yet in later letters in that collection, he says he could not write a play to save his life (92) and that "all the children who have written to me see at once who Aslan is, and grownups never do!" (114). The statements about children and grownups are both wrong, as can easily be seen in collections of Lewis's letters.

It's worth digressing a moment to make the point that sometimes Lewis forgets what his books contain or exaggerates a point because occasionally scholars point to something Lewis said about the series as conclusive proof. But like any other person, he can be fallible or hyperbolic. And when, as is often the case, scholars point to something that another person (most frequently Walter Hooper) says Lewis said, we have even more opportunity for error to occur. These memory and communication breakdowns contribute to widespread confusion among Lewis scholars over a variety of issues that would seem reasonably clear-cut. One example: When and in what order did Lewis write the Chronicles? Virtually all Lewis scholars who write about this disagree with one another, and I myself disagree with all of them! If dating issues interest you, and if you are a detail-oriented person who enjoys complex logic problems, see Appendix C.

So in a clear breaking of the rule about Aslan never telling anyone else's story, Digory is told Jadis's story, that she has indeed gained eternal life. But Aslan notes that "length of days with an evil heart is only length of misery" (174). This echoes God's comment to Christ in *Paradise Lost* (11.60) that death was a blessing for humanity because once innocence was lost, having immortality "serv'd but to eternize woe" (Milton 434).

The other repeated rule of the series is broken on the next page, when Digory is told what would have happened if his mother had eaten the fruit. Aslan says, "It would have healed her; but not to your joy or hers. The day would have come when both you and she would have looked back and said it would have been better to die in that illness" (175).

In the final chapter Aslan tells Polly and Digory that a "Deplorable Word" equivalent may soon appear on our planet, an obvious reference to the atomic bomb, and that "great nations in your world will be ruled by tyrants" (178), an equally obvious reference to countries such as Nazi Germany and the Soviet Union (ruled at that time by Stalin). Then Lewis closes by explaining how events in *Nephew* led to events in *Lion,* a marvelous feat of creativity since the causes had to be created after the effects.

*Nephew* is the most widely allusive of the seven Chronicles, and perhaps there may be value in considering why. It is, in essence, a creation myth; thus Lewis is able to work in aspects of creation stories from Norse, Greek, and Hebrew sources. It's also a story of the fall of humanity (in this case a near fall), which opens up for Lewis's use, in addition to the Bible, large portions of *Paradise Lost.* Finally, in some ways it's a story of Lewis's childhood since in various features Digory Kirke parallels the young Lewis; that brings in biographical elements. So this novel has clear reason to include almost everything Lewis liked, and thus it has a wider variety of allusive elements than any of the other novels.

# CHAPTER 8

# "Further Up and Further In": Allusions in *The Last Battle*

Numerous biblical passages refer to the end-times as the "last days," and Lewis thus reveals the nature of *The Last Battle* right at the beginning when he opens it by referring to "the last days of Narnia" (1). *Battle* closes the series, and like *Lion,* which opens the series in the traditional numbering, its chief source is the Bible, especially end-times passages such as the book of Revelation and the twenty-fifth chapter of Matthew. Whereas Revelation is notoriously opaque, however, Lewis makes *Battle* a much more forthright book, as can be seen from the transparent names of the first two characters to appear—the shifty ape Shift and the perpetually confused donkey Puzzle. The novel significantly begins at the "western end of Narnia" where there "were very few Talking Beasts" (1–2); this symbolizes distance from Aslan, whose country is in the East and whose "holy places" and servants traditionally are located in and come from that direction.

This being a novel of end-times in the biblical sense, one would anticipate Lewis having an Antichrist, and that role is fulfilled, at least initially, by Shift. In one way, of course, Puzzle could be seen as an Antichrist, since it is he who actually wears the lion skin. But Shift is the actual deceiver and leader, fulfilling the role more fully. Since the Antichrist role in the Bible would not entirely work for

Lewis's purposes, however, he needed to find a model for Shift somewhere else, and he seems to have received some useful hints from George Orwell's antitotalitarian novel, *Animal Farm.*

Lewis and Orwell (whose real name was Eric Blair) shared several characteristics. Close contemporaries, being born five years apart and dying in consecutive decades, they were two of Britain's leading writers at mid-century. They shared a hatred of totalitarianism and a love of linguistics and language, seen in Orwell most clearly in the "Newspeak" section of *1984* and in his well-known essay "Politics and the English Language." Not only did each of them have a political novel published in 1945, but they gave their novels strikingly similar subtitles. Lewis called *That Hideous Strength* "A Fairy Tale for Grown-ups," and Orwell labeled *Animal Farm* "A Fairy Story." Today *1984* is Orwell's better-known work, but Lewis preferred *Animal Farm,* and since it appeared in 1945, he was familiar with both it and *1984* (published in 1948) by the time he wrote *Battle* in the early 1950s. We need not rely solely on guesswork to reach that conclusion, since Lewis published an article on January 8, 1955, comparing *Animal Farm* and *1984,* a subject which he said had "exercised [his] mind for a considerable time" (*On Stories* 101).

Since this relatively unfamiliar essay provides the base for the following paragraphs, I provide significant excerpts here:

> What puzzles me is the marked preference of the public for *1984.* For it seems to me (apart from its magnificent, and fortunately detachable, Appendix on "Newspeak") to be merely a flawed, interesting book; but the *Farm* is a work of genius. . . . Paradoxically, when Orwell turns all his characters into animals he makes them more fully human. . . . The greed and cunning of the pigs is tragic (not merely odious) because we are made to care about all the honest, well-meaning, or even heroic beasts whom they exploit. . . . This is what humanity is like; very good, very bad, very pitiable, very honorable (*On Stories* 101, 103, 104).

*Animal Farm* is a political novel tracing the evolution of communism in the Soviet Union; for example, Napoleon and Snowball, the two leading pigs of *Animal Farm,* represent Stalin and Trotsky. Numerous critics have noted the Soviet parallels in the book. But for Lewis a more important attraction was the presentation of an animal becoming ascendant over other animals. While it is difficult to determine to what extent Lewis might have borrowed from Orwell, it is at least intriguing to note several parallels between Shift in *Battle* and the porcine leaders of *Animal Farm.* Shift begins wearing clothes; he walks on two legs rather than four; he makes the other animals serve him; he wears weapons; he perpetually creates new work for the other animals to do; he becomes more authoritative and less frequently seen as time passes; he takes up drinking; and he continually tells the other animals he is doing all this for their own good and that they will be living in a land that is better because of it. All of these actions are taken as well by Napoleon in *Animal Farm.* Perhaps some of these likenesses are simply a feature of any animal taking power over other animals, but the exceptional number of similarities would seem to indicate some debt of Lewis to Orwell.

We see, too, that Lewis included the things he praised Orwell for, such as presenting the suffering of the good-hearted animals in a way to make the novel tragic rather than simply repulsive. The fact that Lewis liked what Orwell did indicates Lewis would probably have written something similar himself. But certainly when an author (and especially the receptive Lewis) has before him a recent example of almost exactly what he is trying to do, he will tend to imitate it (if he admires it) or distance himself from it (if he dislikes it). Since Lewis admired *Animal Farm* so much, and since the leader exaltation is so similar to *Battle,* it seems some imitation took place.

The same can be argued regarding Lewis's and Orwell's similar use of word redefinition by a totalitarian regime. In *Animal Farm* the Seven Commandments undergo gradual change and finally metamorphose into a single commandment which directly opposes the original seven. Lewis does something similar in *Battle,* where Shift says to the other animals, "What do you know about freedom?

You think freedom means doing what you like. Well, you're wrong. That isn't true freedom. True freedom means doing what I tell you" (30–31). Who can read this without being reminded of Orwell's line "freedom is slavery," especially when on the next page Lewis has Shift say, "Tash is Aslan: Aslan is Tash"? As noted above, although Lewis did not greatly like *1984,* he thought the linguistic part was superb. The extent of the debt remains unclear, but definitely George Orwell's writing had an influence on *Battle.*

When Tirian calls on Aslan (prayer) and the helpers of Aslan (a form of invoking the aid of saints), he appears in England in a sort of visionary appearance to the group Peter calls "the seven friends of Narnia" (43). Seven is specified as it is the traditional biblical number of completion, perhaps originally from the seven days of the week. This usage appears most often in Revelation, where there are repeated references to seven angels, seven churches, seven vials, and so on. The favoring of seven continued through medieval times, when the church had Seven Deadly Sins and Seven Acts of Mercy.

Eustace Scrubb and Jill Pole are allowed to enter Narnia in response to Tirian's plea, and from that point until the three of them are thrown through the stable door, approximately eighty pages, is the longest portion of the entire series that is virtually free of allusion. Why does this occur? It is a section dealing with the end of the world, which naturally eliminates biographical possibilities. In Norse mythology, the forces of evil face the forces of good at the final battle of Ragnarok, so initially this would seem a workable source for allusions. But it must be remembered that the main characters in the final Norse conflict are the gods and the frost giants; humans are too weak to be involved in any significant way. And a more serious objection is that Ragnarok ends with the defeat of the gods, obviously not an ending that Lewis can work with in this context. Greek mythology is fuzzy on the subject of end times; it was a subject about which the philosophers talked more than the dramatists and mythmakers. When one is dealing with the future, that limits archaic and obsolete words from linguistics. Mainstream British literature has few works dealing in any detail with the last days.

Of Lewis's six main sources, then, that leaves only the Bible, which Lewis indeed used to some extent in actually bringing an end to Narnia. But for this particular portion, in which good and evil have a closing battle, the Bible is extremely limited as far as details are concerned. While it indicates good will defeat evil at the end of time, there is no detailed commentary regarding how this will take place; instead there is figurative language regarding beasts and dragons—at least, it would have seemed clearly figurative to Lewis. Apocalyptic visions of multiheaded beasts hardly fit a book for children lacking that frame of reference. So the shift in this section away from his usual allusive style is not a deliberate change in style so much as a simple lack of useful sources with which to work.

During the final battle between the Calormenes and the loyal Narnians, one of the most valiant of the Narnians is Jewel the Unicorn, who uses his horn to stab enemy soldiers. This is part of what appears to be an odd coincidence, the number of parallels between *Battle* and George Chapman's Renaissance tragedy *Bussy D'Ambois*. Lewis was not generally enthusiastic about drama, except for Shakespeare. But naturally he would have been familiar with Chapman's work, since the sixteenth century was much of Lewis's scholarly focus, and it is worth noting some surprising similarities between Lewis's novel and Chapman's play. In the first acts of *Bussy*, Chapman speaks of "apes, disfigur'd with the attires of men" (1.2.50), "the ass, stalking in the lion's case, [that] bare himself like a lion" (1.2.201–2), and "an angry young unicorn in his full career" (2.1.119) that kills someone with his horn (Brooke and Paradise 331, 332, 334). In the space of a few pages, then, we have images of Shift, Puzzle, and Jewel. I feel almost certain Lewis did not intend allusions to *Bussy* during the writing of *Battle,* because when Lewis alludes to literature, he virtually always uses works he likes, and I do not know of him ever referring positively to *Bussy.* Therefore (unless Lewis was a fan of Chapman's play and simply never wrote that anywhere) this is either a remarkable coincidence or a case of what Lewis, in the episode referred to in chapter 1, called bits of literature that "pop up uninvited."

After the final battle between good and evil on Narnia, King Tirian is thrust through the stable door and finds himself in the presence of the seven friends of Narnia, now seven kings and queens of Narnia. In this section Lewis does something highly unusual for him; instead of borrowing from his adult books to make a theological point, what I have called autography, he actually writes in opposition to his own beliefs as stated in the adult books. Such an uncharacteristic act, a sort of deliberate nonallusion, or antiallusion, to his own works, merits a closer look.

When Tirian goes through the stable door into Aslan's country, he suddenly recognizes the youngest of the queens:

It was Jill: but not Jill as he had last seen her with her face all dirt and tears and an old drill dress half slipping off one shoulder. Now she looked cool and fresh, as fresh as if she had just come from bathing. . . . Tirian suddenly felt awkward about coming among these people with the blood and dust and sweat of a battle still on him. Next moment he realized that he was not in that state at all. He was fresh and cool and clean, and dressed in such clothes as he would have worn for a great feast at Cair Paravel. (133)

The combination of clothing, cleanliness, and death is familiar to students of Lewis; he uses it in his adult writing in exactly the opposite fashion: "I believe in Purgatory. . . . Would it not break the heart if God said to us, 'It is true, my son, that your breath smells and your rags drip with mud and slime, but we are charitable here and no one will upbraid you with these things, nor draw away from you. Enter into the joy'? Should we not reply, 'With submission, sir, and if there is no objection, I'd rather be cleaned first'" (*Malcolm* 108–9).

But in *Battle* the idea of purgatory is clearly cast aside; Tirian and Jill immediately are cleaned and comfortable in the presence of heavenly beings. Why is there such a contradiction between Lewis's adult and children's writing here?

It is not because his mind changed. Lewis supported the idea of purgatory his whole adult Christian life, and *Letters to Malcolm,* from which the excerpt above is taken, was written approximately a decade after *Battle*. (In passing, it is interesting to note that the children are not perfect upon arriving in Aslan's country; on page 142, Lewis points out that Eustace still had his bad habit of interrupting, and on page 144 Eustace loses his temper. These imperfections would seem to indicate that some sort of purification process is still needed, such as a purgatory might provide.) Nor does the contradiction between Lewis's adult and children's writing occur because of anything heretical. The Anglican Church in Lewis's day did not have a specific position on purgatory.

In fact, it is this optional approach that may have caused Lewis to leave it out. In his books of evangelism and apologetics, such as *Mere Christianity, Miracles,* and *The Problem of Pain,* Lewis tried to stick exclusively to the elements of Christianity which had been accepted by nearly all believers in nearly all times. In his writings directed exclusively toward Christians, such as church papers, private letters, and *Letters to Malcolm,* he felt freer to make his individualistic theology known.

With The Chronicles of Narnia, however, Lewis realized he was writing to a mixed audience. In some ways the tales could be considered a sort of pre-evangelism, and under those circumstances Lewis was always careful to avoid side issues. In addition, the age and maturity of his audience may have been a factor. Lewis probably felt it unwise to present a nonessential theological point disagreeing with the theology of many of his readers' parents.

As the creatures of Narnia come to Aslan for their final judgment, they "all look[ed] straight in his face" (153), thus experiencing the traditional beatific or miserific vision, the medieval idea that at judgment every person sees the face of God in a pleasing or horrifying way. The evil creatures depart to Aslan's left; the good creatures to his right. This accords with the biblical parting of the "sheep and goats" (good and evil) of Matthew 25:33: "And he shall set the sheep on his right hand, but the goats on the left." In fact, in this chapter ("Night Falls on Narnia," a title Lewis at one point thought of using for the entire book), Lewis repeatedly uses the "right hand" motif; the friends of Narnia stand "beside Aslan, on his right side" (149); the stars that have faithfully served Aslan land "a little to the right" (151).

When Narnia ends, Aslan tells Peter to shut the door to it, and Peter "took out a golden key and locked it" (157). It will be remembered from *Lion* that Peter Pevensie sustains many parallels with the apostle Peter, and this is one of them. The Scripture being used here is Matthew 16:19a, in which Christ has just given Peter his name and adds, "And I will give unto thee the keys of the kingdom of heaven."

Then comes the story of Emeth, the righteous Calormene. Emeth tells of his decision to look upon the face of Tash, "though he should slay me" (163), an echo of Job's comment about God in Job 13:15a: "Though he slay me, yet will I trust in him." Lewis's biblical justification for saving Emeth comes from Matthew 7:18 and 21–22a: "A good tree cannot bring forth evil fruit, neither can a corrupt tree bring forth good fruit. . . . Not every one that saith unto me, Lord, Lord, shall enter into the kingdom of heaven; but he that doeth the will of my Father which is in heaven. Many will say to me in that day, Lord, Lord, have we not prophesied in thy name?"

The corresponding passage from *Battle* reads this way: "Therefore if any man swear by Tash and keep his oath for the oath's sake, it is by me that he has truly sworn, though he know it not, and it is I who reward him. And if any man do a cruelty in my name, then though he says the name Aslan, it is Tash whom he serves and by Tash his deed is accepted" (165).

Not only do the thoughts match, but Lewis makes the allusion clear with "in my name" to parallel the biblical "in thy name."

During the telling of Emeth's story, Lewis slyly brings in a piece of clever wordplay. Emeth refers to himself as merely a dog, and one of the dogs immediately takes offense. An older dog excuses Emeth, pointing out:

"'After all, we call our puppies, *Boys,* when they don't behave properly.'

"'So we do,' said the first Dog, 'Or, *girls.*'

"'S-s-sh!' said the Old Dog. 'That's not a nice word to use. Remember where you are'" (166).

The reference, of course, is to humans using the word "bitch" as a vulgar term, so Lewis hypothesizes dogs using the term *girl* as a swear word.

The seven friends of Narnia come to realize that they are in the "real" Narnia and that the Narnia they had first known was merely an image or picture of reality. Digory (who perpetually parallels Lewis in the series) explains it to the others by using the word *shadow*. He says the first Narnia was "only a shadow or a copy of the real Narnia" and that where they are now is as different from the first land "as a real thing is from a shadow" (169). To make the reference explicit, Digory concludes by saying, "It's all in Plato, all in Plato" (170). Lewis, with some rhetorical flourish, once wrote, "To lose what I owe to Plato and Aristotle would be like the amputation of a limb" (*Rehabilitations* 64). One of those debts is the shadow analogy used here. As Lewis expresses it in his Oxford literary history volume, "The natural universe is, for Plato, a world of shadows" (*Oxford* 386). For Plato, any table on earth is an imperfect attempt to copy the ideal table, the perfect table, that exists only in heaven. Plato is thus the source for Aslan's statement near the end of the Chronicles that our world is the "Shadow-lands," a statement famous for its use as the title of the movie, play, and video about Lewis's life. Lewis's statement about the importance of the philosophers to him is not too exaggerated; after all, *Lion* begins the series and *Battle* ends the series with a Lewis figure proclaiming that an understanding of Plato would lead to insight.

In the sixteenth chapter of *Battle* occurs an interesting example of how Lewis, with his remarkable memory for other people's works, would sometimes forget what was contained in his own. Near the start of the chapter occurs this interesting exchange:

"'Isn't it wonderful?' said Lucy. 'Have you noticed one can't feel afraid, even if one wants to? Try it.'

"'By Jove, one can't,' said Eustace after he had tried" (173).

But then just a few pages later when the friends of Narnia face the golden gates, "none of them was bold enough to try if the gates would open" (176). So clearly Lewis can make inaccurate statements regarding the content of his own books, a point of some importance regarding other matters.

The golden gates form part of a wall around a garden, with branches of fruit trees hanging over the sides. The similarity of this description to the garden Digory visited in *Nephew* indicates that this heavenly garden is the reality of which the Narnian garden was the shadow, another piece of Platonism. You will recall from the last chapter that the garden of *Nephew*, going against all the streams of tradition, contained silver apples rather than golden. Why? Lewis, it seems likely, is trying to distinguish the shadow (Narnian) Tree of Life, with green leaves and silver apples, from the real (heavenly) Tree of Life, with silver leaves and golden apples. In effect, he is using the tradition of the book of Revelation, where golden streets and emerald walls are used to convey ultimate value; the key way available for Lewis to show the heavenly tree as the real one is to give it more valuable materials.

The friends of Narnia find Reepicheep, who has indeed made it to Aslan's country; he parallels the biblical figures of Enoch and Elijah, who arrived at heaven without passing through death first. They all notice "that the place was far larger than it had seemed from outside" (178), a concept Lewis borrowed from his own adult novel *The Great Divorce*. Then everyone meets "a King and Queen so great and beautiful that everyone bowed down before them. And well they might, for these two were King Frank and Queen Helen from whom all the most ancient Kings of Narnia and Archenland are descended. And Tirian felt as you would feel if you were brought before Adam and Eve in all their glory" (179).

Lewis had used these same ceremonial elements to close *Perelandra*. The comparison to Adam and Eve at the end directs us to Dante's *Paradiso* for the source of this episode. At first it seems odd for the others to bow down before Frank and Helen, especially such major figures as Peter and Lucy, who were around at Aslan's resurrection. If they parallel Peter and John, and Helen and Frank parallel Adam and Eve, we tend to think of the apostles as outranking Adam and Eve. But in the *Paradiso,* Lewis's guide here, such is not the case. Saved Old Testament figures, such as Solomon, David, and Hezekiah, tend to appear in the middle cantos. The Virgin Mary and Peter have a higher rank, appearing in canto 23; John ranks even higher, in canto 25. But canto 26 is reserved for Adam, who thus has the highest rank of any mortal figure, being the last human being seen before Dante enters the *primum mobile,* the realm of God. In Dante's hierarchy Adam is a more majestic figure than Peter or John; therefore Frank, Lewis's "Adam," is the one before whom all others bow, with Helen attaining equal rank as his consort.

The final paragraph of the Chronicles leaves the good Narnian figures by asserting that "the things that began to happen after that were so great and beautiful that I cannot write them" (183–84). This echoes the final paragraph of the Gospel accounts: "And there are also many other things which Jesus did, the which, if they should be written every one, I suppose that even the world itself could not contain the books that should be written. Amen" (John 21:25). Characteristically, Lewis ends the series by echoing his most common source, the Bible.

As noted earlier, to some extent Lewis's use of allusions depends on the amount of material he has available. In *Nephew,* he had numerous sources to use; in *Battle,* he had few. Readers should not be misled by the lack of allusions in *Battle* into thinking Lewis's fertility was running out or that he was altering his style. To the end of the series, Lewis incorporated parallels and allusions.

CHAPTER 9

# Allusions and the Future of Narnia

As I have suggested, C. S. Lewis was one of the most allusive writers of the twentieth century, and the Chronicles certainly typify his style in that regard. His chief source for allusions in the Chronicles, by a considerable margin, is the Bible. His other sources, in more-or-less descending order, are literature, foreign languages/earlier forms of English, biographical events, Norse mythology, Greco-Roman mythology, autography (borrowings from his adult nonfiction), history, philosophy, and current events. As one might expect, in literature and language his most common borrowings come from the sixteenth and seventeenth centuries. Foreign languages he borrows from include Latin, Hebrew, Old Norse, French, Turkish, Spanish, and Greek. (More accurately, these are the ones I recognize; if Lewis borrowed from, say, Urdu, I would never know it.) If one were to try to determine the main influence on each book (which is difficult to do), probably *Lion*, *Nephew*, and *Battle* are the most biblical; *Chair* and *Horse* the most biographical; *Treader*, the most literary; and *Caspian*, the most linguistic.

An interesting feature of Lewis's use of allusions is his subtlety. Seldom are the allusions overt. Often they create an impression on the reader, as with "Tarkaan," without awareness of how the spell is being woven.

The Chronicles of Narnia has been an enormously successful series for the past fifty years; how likely is this success to continue? It is risky to predict, but I believe the Chronicles will continue to generate much popular appreciation and critical attention for many years to come.

Two main factors should keep the Chronicles popular over the coming decades. First, in the children's literature field, works of fantasy tend to sustain their popularity longer than works of contemporary realism. Many successful children's books of the past seem at first glance to be contemporary realism: the works of Louisa May Alcott, Laura Ingalls Wilder, and Mark Twain, for instance. But these are actually books of historical realism rather than of contemporary realism. When Twain and Wilder write their novels, they are reflecting back on their own childhoods, not writing a children's novel in a contemporary setting.

When realistic children's novels are placed in a contemporary setting, that choice usually means the illustrations, dialogue, and references must be updated from time to time to ensure the book's contemporaneity. If the book is part of a series, the authors can simply update the characters and situations on a continual basis, as has been the case with Nancy Drew. Even then, however, sometimes sheer embarrassment forces the producers of a series to rewrite the earlier titles, as with the long-running Bobbsey Twins series, around since the First World War. In the rewrites of those early works, Dinah is no longer a "colored" maid who says, "I'se agwine to go"; she is now a paid black worker who speaks standard English. Since the Chronicles are primarily set in another world, they will not grow outdated as rapidly as novels set in our own.

Also, with fantasy works, readers are more forgiving of quirks in setting and situation; they approach the novel ready to suspend disbelief. The discrepancies in the Chronicles are not the bar to reader involvement that they could be in a realistic series.

The other key factor which should maintain popularity for the Chronicles among general audiences is the theological content. Adults may remember children's novels with affection, but in a world where the saying from Ecclesiastes about endless bookmaking is ever truer, most adults have little time or inclination to return to childhood reading. The Chronicles are an exception, however; repeatedly one meets adults who have reread the works as grownups, and most often the reason is the theological content. This means, of course, that these adults already have the books around the house for their own children, read the books (if they are elementary teachers) to a new generation, and introduce the series to adult friends in homes and churches. With the audience so continually replenished, the Chronicles seem likely to remain popular for many decades.

As for critical attention, the Chronicles will likely continue to receive a great deal of that as well, perhaps more so than any other series of children's books. Again, two main reasons contribute to this.

Most children's books fit only into a course on children's books. Even with canonical loosening, it is hard to see where, say, *Tales of a Fourth Grade Nothing* by Judy Blume might be studied in a college English department except in a children's literature course. The Chronicles, on the other hand, have been taught under a variety of genres. Besides their "natural" place in children's literature, the Chronicles fit readily into courses on C. S. Lewis, the Inklings, fantasy literature, and religious literature. The books are read in both English departments and religion departments. For books to receive scholarly attention, they must first be read by people operating within academic settings, and this will continue to be the case for the Chronicles.

More significantly, the Chronicles will generate more scholarly attention than other children's books because of Lewis's "layered" approach. Most children's novels can be written about in traditional terms such as plot, character, theme, conflict, and so on. In addition, children's novels invite attention toward their readability and teachability—articles on classroom approaches, for instance.

But the Chronicles, because of Lewis's allusions and parallels, will generate critical interest for years to come. Some critics will discover, as this study has, new allusions and parallels. Other writers will delve further, discerning how Lewis altered and transformed his sources, finding patterns and habits. Still other scholars will compare Lewis's allusive style in his children's works to the writing of his adult novels and nonfiction. It can be said of Lewis what John Dryden observed of Chaucer, that we have game springing up everywhere before us; and numberless bushes in the Chronicles have not yet been sufficiently beaten to reveal all their quarry.

Roger Green and Walter Hooper said their biography of Lewis was *a* biography, not *the* biography. One could question whether *the* biography of Lewis (or any other literary figure) can ever be written. And this book is not *the* study on allusions; it is *a* study, a helpful start. When other critics point out, as they will, sources and parallels this book has overlooked, I shall be not dismayed but pleased. At the very least this study should provoke useful discussion of some broader issues; why, for example, should Lewis, such a defender of traditional values and expressions, have been so strongly repelled by the book of Proverbs? This book has not been, in general, an attempt to wrestle with large issues but an effort at laying a foundation on which others may build; for recognizing the depth and variety of allusions used by C. S. Lewis in The Chronicles of Narnia is one key to understanding and appreciating the style in which he wrote.

Besides, finding out about allusions is fun! I hope you've enjoyed the journey.

APPENDIX A

# A Brief Background of C. S. Lewis

Clive Staples Lewis, author of The Chronicles of Narnia, was born a little over a century ago, in 1898, in Belfast, Northern Ireland. That part of Ireland has for years been a land where political and theological differences are deeply felt and hotly debated. Perhaps this divisiveness contributed to Lewis's becoming virtually apolitical and atheistic during his teen years.

His was a bookish family, and young Lewis (known from the age of four as "Jack," at his own request) took full advantage of the literary opportunities surrounding him. As he put it in his autobiography: "I am a product of . . . endless books. . . . In the seemingly endless rainy afternoons I took volume after volume from the shelves. I had always the same certainty of finding a book that was new to me as a man who walks into a field has of finding a new blade of grass" (Surprised 10).

Lewis read children's stories as well as adult fiction; he particularly enjoyed the works of Beatrix Potter, Edith Nesbitt, and Conan Doyle (Green and Hooper 21). His pleasure in these stories led him to try creating his own "Animal-Land," where "chivalrous mice and rabbits . . . rode out in complete mail to kill not giants but cats" (*Surprised* 13). This sounds, on the surface, like an earlier version of Narnia; but Lewis in his autobiography warns readers that "Animal-Land had nothing whatever in common with Narnia except the anthropomorphic beasts" (*Surprised* 15). His brother Warren, two years older, enjoyed history and wrote stories about India; the Lewis brothers therefore combined their real and mythical countries into one realm, Boxen. They continued discussing and, in Jack's case, writing and drawing about this kingdom for several years.

When Lewis was nine, his mother died of cancer; the emotional pain seemed to affect Jack for the rest of his life. Shortly afterward he had to go off to boarding school for the first time. A series of unpleasant school experiences darkened his outlook and gave him perhaps a more pessimistic view of human nature than he might otherwise have had.

After some years, however, Lewis at last achieved congenial educational surroundings when he went to stay with William Kirkpatrick, a friend of his father's, who tutored Lewis in preparation for a hoped-for scholarship to Oxford. The scholarship eventually came about, with only Lewis's inability to pass the required math exam between him and his future academic career. World War I intervened, and England's hardship was Lewis's gain; he served in the war as a volunteer, and afterwards a grateful country exempted its soldiers from university qualifying exams, including in Lewis's case the math exam. He took undergraduate and graduate degrees at Oxford (the latter in both Philosophy and Literature), and finally in 1925, at the age of twenty-six, he became a literature don (similar to a college professor here) at Magdalen College, Oxford. (The preceding sentence, by the way, illustrates what I call "The Rule of One": Since Lewis was born near the end of 1898, for almost any event in his life, you can find his age by adding one to the year. When World War II began in 1939, Jack was 40; when he married Joy in 1956, he was 57.)

Lewis had by 1925 published two volumes of poetry, today rarely read. After a decade of relative literary dryness, he finally achieved academic stature in the mid-1930s with his monumental volume of literary criticism, *The Allegory of Love*. In the 1940s he added to his fame with publications in a variety of fields: literary criticism (*A Preface to Paradise Lost*), apologetics/religion (*Mere Christianity, The Problem of Pain*), and science fiction (*Perelandra*). His religious novel *The Screwtape Letters*, a 1942 top-ten best seller in England, contributed to his recognition in the United States as well; in 1947 Lewis appeared on the cover of *Time*. In the 1950s he moved into children's fantasy with The Chronicles of Narnia and mythological fiction with *Till We Have Faces*. During this period Lewis became professor of medieval and Renaissance literature at Cambridge. By the time of his death on November 22, 1963 (coincidental with the deaths of Aldous Huxley and John F. Kennedy), Lewis had published a collection of works that continues to sell millions of copies each year.

APPENDIX B

# What Are Allusions, and How Important Are They?

Since this book uses the term *allusion* many times, perhaps I should explain what I mean by the term. An allusion is a reference (direct or indirect) to something else, which could be anything from an event to a person to a famous saying to a work of literature. Its effective use is considered linguistically clever; in fact, the word *allusion* comes from Latin *allusio,* which means "a playing with." Here are some examples of allusions:

ORIGINAL: You can lead a horse to water, but you can't make it drink.

ALLUSION: You can lead a student to class, but you can't make him think.

ORIGINAL: The best-laid schemes o' mice and men (a line from Robert Burns' poem "To a Mouse").

ALLUSION: *Of Mice and Men* (novel by John Steinbeck).

ALLUSION: "Of Headless Mice . . . and Men" (*Time* essay on cloning by Charles Krauthammer).

As you can see, the allusion sometimes borrows from the original exactly; more often it takes a portion of the original and alters it or adds to it. Sometimes allusions can even be semiprivate. Suppose a family has a bad experience with greasy floors at a place called Hot Dog Heaven. If someone suggests eating at an untested fast-food restaurant, a family member may respond, "What are their floors like?" Everyone in the family will laugh at that remark, but a person without the shared experience misses the humorous point. An allusion, then, is intended to trigger remembrance; it's a verbal reminder.

This book generally uses *allusion, borrowing,* and *reference* to refer to elements of the Chronicles that seem clearly traceable to a source or sources. Other terms, such as *parallel, analogue,* and *correspondence,* will signify elements more connected to exterior writings and events by similarity than by actual reference. No book-length studies of Lewis so far have focused on allusions; in fact, some Lewis critics have distanced themselves from "source hunting." Occasionally they seem to feel this sort of thing beneath them-. selves. They overlook the fact that Lewis himself did source studies; in "The Genesis of a Medieval Book," from *Studies in Medieval and Renaissance Literature,* Lewis shows for a series of works how the medieval writer Layamon borrowed from another writer named Wace, and Wace, in turn, from a third author, Geoffrey of Monmouth.

How important is it to study the allusions, sources, and parallels for the Chronicles? Some critics have said that locating Lewisian sources is, at best, a trivial activity; at worst, a fruitless waste of time that keeps one from engaging in "real" scholarly endeavor. Peter Schakel, author of the Narnia study *Reading with the Heart,* speaks for this group in saying "the sources of Lewis's ideas . . . are of little importance . . . they should not be needed and might encourage readers to intellectualize the Chronicles, rather than enter them imaginatively" (xii).

But what happens if scholars fail to engage in accurate and useful source and parallel studies? General readers of the Chronicles will still realize that Lewis is referring to various events or readings and will naturally wonder what those are. Questions about sources and allusions will not go unasked. As Schakel admits, these questions are "frequently asked" (xi). Questions that are frequently asked will be answered, or at least answers will be attempted, and the real choice is therefore not between recognizing allusions or ignoring them but between presenting accurate or inaccurate answers, useful or misleading responses.

We can see clearly what happens when a scholar doesn't know Lewis's sources by examining David Holbrook's book on Narnia (published by a university press) entitled *The Skeleton in the Wardrobe*. Since Holbrook is not very well-read in the areas important to Lewis, such as mythology and Renaissance literature, he creates his own false sources and draws erroneous conclusions from them. Here is an example from his discussion of *Lion*: "The faun's name is Tumnus, the origins of which now seem clear: *Tumesco*, to swell; *Tumidas,* big, protuberant; *Tumor,* a bump or bunch; also perhaps *tum* 'at that time': and perhaps just the infant's 'tummy.' Perhaps Tumnus is the father's penis inside the mother which became a cancer?" (68).

But surely a much clearer origin for the name is the last two syllables of the Roman god Vertumnus. The spellings are exactly the same; Lewis derives many Narnian names from mythology; and the other main figure in the Vertumnus myth, Pomona, appears in the Chronicles as well. For the name *Tumnus,* it seems probable an objective judge would consider *Vertumnus* a more likely source than *tumor*. (For more on how the name *Vertumnus* relates to *Lion,* see chapter 2 of the text.) Because Holbrook is (it appears) unfamiliar with Vertumnus, he scatters his psychological seed far and wide to find a source, and he does indeed raise a linguistic crop; but the plants seem to be mostly weeds.

Holbrook provides other examples of far-fetched allusions. He suggests *mustache* as the name-source for the Calormene god Tash, for instance. Since a mustache has stiff hair, that leads Holbrook (in his usual insistently Freudian way) to think of pubic hair, and so the name Tash eventually turns into, as one would expect from a Freudian reader, subliminal evidence for Lewis's (alleged) fear of human sexuality. Holbrook believes the name *Hwin* to come from the Houhynhyms of Jonathan Swift's eighteenth-century novel *Gulliver's Travels*, overlooking the fact that *Hwin*, like *Bree*, is simply a shortened form of a noise horses make. The spelling of *Hwin* is much closer to *whinny* than to *Houhynhym*, and when we remember that in Lewis's beloved Anglo-Saxon English *h* precedes *w* (as in the opening word *hwaet* of *Beowulf*), we need not apply to *Gulliver* for a source at all.

Going through the derivations step-by-step this way, we can avoid being fooled by Holbrook's created sources. But how many readers have the knowledge of minor Greco-Roman gods and Anglo-Saxon orthography to recognize the true sources? If the true origins are not being sought after and published, will not false origins hold sway, leading to a misunderstanding of the text? We cannot stop Holbrook and others from attempting to sow weeds of allusive confusion, but at the very least we should seed the ground plentifully with good seed and not give up the field of source-study entirely to the weeds.

A second reason for searching after allusions and parallels is inadvertently provided by Lewis biographer Walter Hooper in a paragraph on the limitations of source-hunting. Hooper says that "when a teacher comes across a pupil who rejoices in having solved a mere 'puzzle' . . . the teacher should lead him away from the suspect realm of anthropology to true literary pleasures. . . . It is, for instance, not enough to say that the immediate source of Shakespeare's *Romeo and Juliet* is Arthur Brooke's extremely ugly *Tragical History of Romeus and Juliet*; we need to show him what a completely different use Shakespeare made of the story" (108–9).

Hooper's words *mere* and *suspect* show readily enough where he stands, and the point is, within limits, a fair one. But before showing Shakespeare's use of Arthur Brooke, don't we first have to be aware of Brooke? How many scholars would have heard of the obscure Arthur Brooke without an annotated edition of *Romeo and Juliet* making them aware of his writing? Consider the name *Puddleglum* for the marshwiggle in *Chair*. If Lewis had not indicated in his *Oxford History of English Literature* volume that he had derived that name from obscure sixteenth-century writer John Studley, wouldn't the name be used to support articles on Lewis's originality and fertility of invention? How many critics know the works of Studley well enough to recognize the Puddleglum allusion on their own?

Even if critics are familiar with the works Lewis used, they often, in my judgment, fail to recognize allusions, fail to cite them properly, or otherwise mislead readers who want to know sources. As an example of this, I can use Dr. Paul Ford, founder of the Southern California C. S. Lewis Society, the brilliant author of *Companion to Narnia,* which is described on the cover as a "complete guide" to Narnia, and that phrase is as truthful as publishing blurbs get. Dr. Ford knows Narnia as well as anyone; as a theology professor, we can assume he has a fairly thorough knowledge of the Bible. So how well does the leading scholar of Narnia do in tracing allusions from the Bible? In the following lines I will present (from pages 78–79 of *Companion to Narnia*) Ford's first biblical allusion from each of the first three Chronicles, so you may judge whether the sourcing seems accurate:

Lewis quote: "Daughter of Eve" (*Lion*)

Ford's biblical source: "Wherefore, as by one man sin entered into the world, and death by sin; and so death passed upon all men, for that all have sinned." (Rom. 5:12)

Lewis quote: "The people that lived in hiding." (*Caspian*)

Ford's biblical source: "Nevertheless the dimness shall not be such as was in her vexation, when at the first he lightly afflicted the land of Zebulun and the land of Naphtali, and afterward did more grievously afflict her by the way of the sea, beyond Jordan, in Galilee of the nations." (Isa. 9:1)

Lewis quote: "As bad as I was" (*Treader*)

Ford's biblical source: "Confess your faults one to another, and pray one for another, that ye may be healed. The effectual fervent prayer of a righteous man availeth much." (James 5:16)

These are not even close. I could provide other examples, but these make the point. If perhaps the best Narnian scholar of the past thirty years cannot trace allusions accurately in just one book (the Bible) that he knows well, how can he trace allusions effectively in other books that he presumably knows less well? And that, of course, is the reason for this book's existence: no author has previously presented a thorough, accurate, insightful guide to allusions in Narnia.

If all critics of the Chronicles had complete, in-depth knowledge of Norse mythology and Greco-Roman mythology and the Bible and Middle English and linguistics and the church fathers and Anglo-Saxon and the life of Lewis and Renaissance prose and epic poetry and—but there is, in the case of Lewis, really no place to stop. As is noted in the main section of this book, C. S. Lewis was one of the best-read men of his generation, perhaps *the* best-read, and that is a truly remarkable statement, for his was a well-read generation. If we could assume critics of the Chronicles read everything Lewis read (already the assumption breaks down), and that they remember everything they read, and that they recognize every connection between what Lewis produced and what he read, then the work of the source-hunter would be over, and we could indeed limit ourselves to Hooper's higher calling. But that day will never come, and thus there will always be work for the discoverer of allusions and parallels. Even if we grant cooking to be a higher skill than shopping, unless food is brought to the kitchen for preparation, who can eat?

A final reason for seeking out and presenting allusions and parallels is that the critics who denigrate source studies by others nonetheless engage in source studies repeatedly themselves. Walter Hooper's *Past Watchful Dragons,* despite its warnings against chasing parallels, presents numerous sources and allusions to help illuminate the text. The paragraph quoted above, in which he downplays the importance of sources, itself lists three sources of use to the Narnian critic. Peter Schakel, the critic most vehemently against illuminating the series through source studies, himself turns immediately to sources whenever he fears ignoring them will lead to misreading. Hooper and Schakel warn others away from the feast of sources that they freely delve into; is this because only they know how to appreciate the nourishment there? It seems improper for a scholar to condemn others for enjoying a meal he freely eats of himself.

Without question, then, discovering and revealing allusions is worthwhile scholarly activity. If scholarship involves pursuing truth and revealing knowledge, then to uncover facts that can illuminate a work, or can enable other scholars to illuminate a work, is undoubtedly scholarship, whereas "higher" criticism that obscures the text may not be. Thus, despite the carping and caviling of Hooper, Schakel, and others, this type of study merits respect.

Two key areas for discussion of allusions over the years have been the extent to which the Chronicles can be labeled "allegory," and from what sources Lewis drew his material. This book focuses on the second of those questions, but the first one is significant enough to merit some mention here in an appendix. (Of course, if this issue is of no interest to you, here is your opportunity to return to the main text.)

Lewis himself always fervently denied that the Chronicles were allegories. In a December 24, 1959, letter about *Lion,* he comments: "But it is not, as some people think, an *allegory,* that is, I don't say 'Let us represent Christ as Aslan.' I say, 'Supposing there was a world like Narnia, and supposing, like ours, it needed redemption, let us imagine what sort of Incarnation and Passion and Resurrection Christ would have there.' See?" (*Letters* 486). As this comes from the author of the works themselves, a man who spent much of his career studying and explaining allegory, that would seem to settle it.

But *allegory* is a slippery term, and our answer to the question of whether the Chronicles are allegories may well depend on how the term is defined. As Lewis acknowledged in another letter, "the word [*allegory*] can be used in wider or narrower senses. . . . The truth is it's one of those words which needs defining in each context where one uses it" (*Letters* 461). This explains why J. R. R. Tolkien could condemn *Lion* as allegory while Lewis denied it even fit the category. Certainly Tolkien's works differ from Lewis's in being much more shadowy and elusive regarding connections with our own world and literature. Although readers have sometimes labeled Gandalf in *The Lord of the Rings* a type of Christ figure, he clearly does not fulfill that role to the extent Aslan does in the Chronicles. Aslan is not just a Christ figure in the traditional literary sense, and not just "Christ for Narnia," as is sometimes assumed, but Aslan *is* Christ, the same person in a different world. The Chronicles themselves specify this in the closing pages of *Treader*:

"You are too old, children," said Aslan, "and you must begin to come close to your own world now."

"It isn't Narnia, you know," sobbed Lucy. "It's you. We shan't meet you there. And how can we live, never meeting you?"

"But you shall meet me, dear one," said Aslan.

"Are—are you there too, Sir?" said Edmund.

"I am," said Aslan. "But there I have another name. You must learn to know me by that name. This was the very reason why you were brought to Narnia, that by knowing me here for a little, you may know me better there." (215–16)

It sometimes seems Lewis repeatedly denies the term *allegory* to protect readers from confusing Narnian events with our world's events, but that's a confusion I don't believe readers are liable to make. Instead, I think most readers perceive similarities that they consider "allegorical elements" in the novels; they say, "Ah, this is like the stoning of Stephen in our world!" Lewis allows and contributes to that perception, as in these excerpts from a June 8, 1960, letter:

3.  The stone table is meant to remind one of Moses' table.

      4.   The Passion and Resurrection of Aslan are the Passion and Resurrection Christ might be supposed to have had in that world. . . .

      7.   And of course the Ape and Puzzle, just before the last Judgment (in *The Last Battle*) are like the coming of Antichrist before the end of our world.

All clear? (*Letters to Children* 93)

To find allegorical elements, or similarities, does not at all mean to find equalities. Author Thomas Howard thinks it does; thus he argues strenuously against "chasing parallels," as he puts it: "If we were to claim that there is a significant correspondence between Narnia and the real world, then we have opened up the troublesome topic of allegory, and everyone is off chasing parallels. Aslan equals Christ, the White Witch equals Lilith; Peter equals Saint Peter, and so forth" (34).

This portrays a common and erroneous view that allegory means every incident and character from the created world must have a corresponding incident or character from our world. But Peter in *Lion* can parallel our world's apostle Peter without corresponding in every way; if they corresponded exactly, they would be the same person! (Aslan is indeed the same person in both worlds; but as a transcendent figure who can presumably be in both worlds at once, he belongs in a separate category.)

Perhaps a standard literary example of allegory can clarify this. In John Dryden's allegorical poem *Absalom and Achitophel*, King David clearly represents King Charles II of England, and Absalom just as clearly represents James, Duke of Monmouth. But this does not at all mean Absalom parallels James in every way. The thirty-ninth line of the poem, for instance, discusses Absalom's murder of his half brother Amnon. James never murdered any of his brothers (or half brothers). Yet no reputable critic argues that this discrepancy means Absalom does not provide an allegorical parallel to James in the poem. Allegorical characters are similar to real people in the way state capital buildings resemble one another, by being of the same type; allegorical characters are not like identical documents issuing from the same printer. We can use *Absalom and Achitophel* to provide another clarification as well. Walter Hooper, in *Past Watchful Dragons,* claims allegory means, to both him and Lewis, "the use of something real and tangible to stand for that which is real but intangible. Love can be allegorized, patience can be allegorized, anything immaterial can be allegorized or represented by physical objects. But Aslan, for example, is already a physical object" (129).

Thus, Hooper argues, by definition Aslan cannot be an allegorical figure for Christ, since they are both tangible. But David and Absalom serve as allegorical representations of Charles II and James Monmouth, even though all four are tangible. Lest it seem *Absalom and Achitophel* is a lone exception to the rules of allegory, let us examine a clear and famous example of the type, *Pilgrim's Progress.* In the opening pages of the work, Pilgrim has "a book in his hand, and a great burden upon his back" (*Norton* 1776). Allegorically, the book is the Bible, and the burden is the guilt of sin. In the same sentence, then, allegorical elements are used to stand for tangible (Bible) and intangible (guilt) facets of our world. Pilgrim later meets men named Evangelist (tangible) and Obstinate (Intangible) and visits the Britain Row (tangible) of Vanity Fair (intangible). In Spenser's *Faerie Queene,* among other meanings Gloriana represents (the tangible) Elizabeth I, as Spenser points out in his preface.

In summation, then, while the Chronicles are not merely allegories, they contain allegorical elements. And in portions of the series, especially in *Lion, Treader,* and *Battle,* sufficient allegorical elements are joined together to justify labeling sections of those books allegorical.

APPENDIX C

# Dating the Chronicles

WARNING: This appendix is only for people who are *heavily* into Narnia-related details!

In their edition of Lewis's *Letters to Children,* Lyle Dorsett and Marjorie Mead assert, "Lewis had actually finished writing all of the seven volumes . . . in 1952" (31). Paul Ford in *Companion to Narnia* claims *The Last Battle* was completed in spring 1953 and *The Magician's Nephew* in the early months of 1954 (45). Green and Hooper in their biography of Lewis claim *Battle* was finished in March 1953 and revised and typed in May of that year, with *Nephew* being revised sometime thereafter (248). Humphrey Carpenter follows Green and Hooper regarding *Battle* but dates *Nephew* some two years earlier (227). Is any of these dating systems accurate? I'm inclined to doubt it, but the mass of conflicting evidence makes me wonder whether we can ever solve this problem.

In a letter dated "14ᵗʰ Sept. 1953," Lewis responds to a reader of the Chronicles who apparently disliked the idea of the Pevensie children becoming adults in Narnia while remaining children when they returned to this world. Lewis writes, "I feel sure I'm right to make them grow up in Narnia. Of course they will grow up in this world too. You'll see" (Dorsett and Mead 34).

But the Pevensie children (excluding Susan, whose fate we do not learn) do not grow up in this world. They are killed within a few years of their entry into Narnia. The span of (our world's) time covered from *Lion*, when the Pevensies enter Narnia, to *Battle*, when they die, seems to be three to four years. Thus at their deaths Peter, Edmund, and Lucy are approximately sixteen, thirteen, and twelve, respectively—by no means grown up in the Narnian sense, where they rule as full-fledged adults for several years. In September 1953, therefore, Lewis appears not to have yet determined the conclusion of *Battle*, in which the Pevensies die as children.

Thus all dates before September 1953 for a final copy of *Battle* would be inaccurate, particularly the very early date of 1952, written by Dorsett and Mead. The other dating schemes present more complex problems. Ford and Carpenter both base their dating on a statement in the Green and Hooper biography that Lewis wrote a letter to his publisher on March 11, 1953, saying, "I have just finished the seventh and really the last of the Narnian stories" (248). It was, Green and Hooper assert, "revised and ready to be typed by the end of May" (248). That letter has never been published, to my knowledge, and one would have to see the original to determine the accuracy of the dating and wording. There are reasons to believe Green and Hooper are in some way mistaken, as will be shown here.

It clearly seems wrong to assert that *Battle* was completed in the spring of 1953, when in September of that year Lewis did not yet know how the book ended. One could, in trying to support this dating, argue that Lewis did already know how *Battle* would end and that the Pevensies really did reach adulthood on Earth, as the September letter indicates they would. This appears to be Paul Ford's approach in Appendix 2 of his *Companion to Narnia*, where he claims Peter, Edmund, and Lucy to be twenty-two, nineteen, and seventeen in *Battle*. This chronology assumes seven years elapse between *The Silver Chair* and *The Last Battle*. Yet in *Battle*, Eustace Scrubb says the time between the events of *Chair* and *Battle* was "more than a year ago by our time" (48). Admittedly, seven years is more than a year, but "more than a year" would be an extremely odd way to express "seven years." If a new acquaintance asks whether you have any children, and you say, "Yes, I have a daughter more than a year old," that acquaintance would be surprised if the daughter were a second-grader! Surely a wiser reading would estimate "more than a year" as one to two years.

In addition, Jill Pole and Eustace are repeatedly referred to upon their Narnian return in *Battle* by youthful terms, such as "boy," "girl," "the youngest boy and girl," and "children" (45–48). These words better fit youths around eleven, as I calculate them to be, than Ford's estimate of sixteen. Finally, even if one accepts Ford's assumption that Edmund and Lucy are "grown-ups" as teenagers, Ford's assigning Peter the age of twenty-two in *Battle* is difficult to reconcile with the rest of that book. King Tirian is "between twenty and twenty-five years old," according to the second chapter (12). When he sees Peter, he notes immediately that Peter is "certainly younger" (42) than himself. How could Tirian in his early twenties think of a twenty-two-year-old as noticeably younger than himself?

Ford's estimate of seven years between *Chair* and *Battle* comes from two sources. Internally, Eustace comments in *Battle* that he and Jill are the only two of the seven friends of Narnia "who are still at school" (50). But school can be a nebulous term. For instance, is a person being tutored, as Lewis was with Kirkpatrick, "at school"?

A more serious objection is that Lewis himself, in his outline of Narnian history, supposedly had the interval between *Chair* and *Battle* as seven English years (Hooper 44). This seems at first glance final, but there are reasons for hesitation in accepting this account. Lewis's penmanship in later years was poor, and the outline he handed Hooper was handwritten. It is possible Hooper misread a number and thought a one or two was a seven.

Even if Hooper read the handwriting accurately, however, Lewis's indication of seven years is by no means a fatal objection. As noted in chapter 7, Lewis had a remarkable memory for the literature of others but frequently forgot details in his own works. He once wrote to a reader, "If I had time to re-read my own book . . . I'd be able to answer you better" (*Letters to Children* 96).

Internal evidence seems solidly to indicate that the children in the Chronicles are not full-fledged grown-ups by the time of *The Last Battle.* Since Lewis writes in September 1953 that the Pevensies will be grown-ups in *Battle,* and they are not, Ford's assumption that *Battle* was finished by spring of 1953 must be erroneous.

That leaves, then, the vexing problem of the order in which the books were written. Everyone seems to agree that the first five were finished as follows: *Lion, Caspian, Treader, Horse,* and *Chair.* And apparently almost everyone, with the notable exception of Humphrey Carpenter, has heretofore accepted that *Battle* was completed next, with *Nephew* last. The common view may be right, but in a letter dated March 19, 1954, Lewis indicates *Nephew* went to the printer about the second week of March (Dorsett and Mead 40). A late date of January-March 1954 for completing *Nephew* (Ford's estimate) in handwriting does not allow much time margin if a proofread, typed, and titled manuscript was at the publisher in early March. In addition, *Battle* incorporates events of *Nephew* (such as references to Digory and Polly) as early as the fourth and fifth chapters, which makes one think *Nephew* was written before *Battle* (just as Lewis's inclusion of events from *The Horse and His Boy* in *The Silver Chair* shows that he had already written *Horse*). Of course, Lewis could have written *Battle* first, then written *Nephew,* then rewritten *Battle* to incorporate the events of *Nephew,* but it seems cumbersome to posit an extra step unless absolutely necessary.

One can see why so many differing dates for the composition of the Chronicles have been presented. Part of the evidence comes from unpublished letters and manuscripts which would have to be carefully examined, another part comes from the admittedly flawed memory of Lewis regarding his own works, and a third part involves jumps of logic which are often dictated by various writers' preconceptions, a human failing in which I join. But in conclusion, using evidence from the letters and adding likely conjectures, it appears to me that Lewis completed *Battle* between September 1953 and March 1954 and that he finished *Nephew* somewhat earlier, presumably sometime in 1953.

# Works Cited

Abrams, M. H., et. al., eds. *The Norton Anthology of English Literature.* Vols. 1–2. 3rd ed. New York: Norton, 1974.

Arnold, Matthew. "Dover Beach." Abrams Vol. 2, 1355–56.

"The Battle of Maldon." Abrams Vol. 1, 90–95.

Bevington, David, ed. *The Complete Works of Shakespeare.* New York: Addison-Wesley, 1997.

Boethius. *The Consolation of Philosophy.* Trans. Richard Green. Indianapolis: Bobbs-Merrill, 1962.

Carpenter, Humphrey. *The Inklings.* Boston: Houghton Mifflin, 1979.

Carroll, Lewis. *Alice's Adventures in Wonderland.* New York: Norton, 1971.

Chamberlin, E. R. *Everyday Life in Renaissance Times.* New York: G. P. Putnam's Sons, 1965.

Chapman, George. *Bussy D'Ambois. English Drama 1580–1642.* Ed. C. F. Tucker Brooke and Nathaniel Burton Paradise. New York: D. C. Heath, 1933.

Dante. *The Paradiso.* Trans. John Ciardi. New York: New American Library, 1970.

Davidson, H. R. Ellis. *God and Myths of Northern Europe.* New York: Penguin, 1964.

DiCesare, Mario A., ed. *George Herbert and the Seventeenth-Century Religious Poets.* New York: Norton, 1978.

Doyle, Arthur Conan. *Adventures of Sherlock Holmes.* New York: Lancer, 1968.

Dryden, John. "A Song for St. Cecilia's Day." Abrams Vol. 1, 1749–51.

Ford, Paul. *Companion to Narnia.* 4th ed. New York: HarperCollins, 1994.

Green, Roger, and Walter Hooper. *C. S. Lewis: A Biography.* New York: Harcourt Brace, 1976.

Griffin, William. *Clive Staples Lewis: A Dramatic Life.* New York: Harper and Row, 1986.

Herbert, George. "The Son." DiCesare, 60.

Holbrook, David. *The Skeleton in the Wardrobe.* Lewisburg, N.J.: Bucknell University Press, 1991.

Hooper, Walter. *Past Watchful Dragons.* New York: Macmillan, 1979.

L'Engle, Madeleine. Foreword. *Companion to Narnia.* By Paul Ford. New York: HarperCollins, 1994.

Lewis, C. S. *Christian Reflections.* Ed. Walter Hooper. Grand Rapids: Eerdmans, 1967.

—. *English Literature in the Sixteenth Century Excluding Drama.* Vol. III of the *Oxford History of English Literature.* Oxford: Oxford University Press, 1954.

—. *The Essential C. S. Lewis.* Ed. Lyle W. Dorsett. New York: Macmillan, 1988.

—. *God in the Dock.* Ed. Walter Hooper. Grand Rapids: Eerdmans, 1970.

—. *The Horse and His Boy.* New York: Macmillan, 1954.

—. *The Last Battle.* New York: Macmillan, 1956.

—. *Letters of C. S. Lewis.* Ed. Walter Hooper. Rev. ed. New York: Harcourt Brace, 1988.

—. *Letters to an American Lady.* Ed. Clyde S. Kilby. Grand Rapids: Eerdmans, 1971.

—. *Letters to Children.* Ed. Lyle W. Dorsett and Marjorie Lamp Mead. New York: Macmillan, 1985.

—. *Letters to Malcolm.* New York: Harcourt Brace, 1963.

—. *The Lion, the Witch and the Wardrobe.* New York: Macmillan, 1950.

—. *The Magician's Nephew.* New York: Macmillan, 1955.

—. *Mere Christianity.* Rev. ed. New York: Macmillan, 1952.

—. *On Stories.* Ed. Walter Hooper. New York: Harcourt Brace, 1982.

— and E. M. W. Tillyard. *The Personal Heresy.* London: Oxford University Press, 1939.

—. *Prince Caspian.* New York: Macmillan, 1951.

—. *The Problem of Pain.* New York: Macmillan, 1940.

—. *The Quotable Lewis.* Ed. Wayne Martindale and Jerry Root. Wheaton, Ill.: Tyndale House, 1989.

—. *Reflections on the Psalms.* New York: Harcourt Brace, 1958.

—. *The Silver Chair.* New York: Macmillan, 1953.

—. *Studies in Medieval and Renaissance Literature.* Ed. Walter Hooper. Cambridge: Cambridge University Press, 1966.

—. *Surprised by Joy.* New York: Harcourt Brace, 1954.

—. *The Voyage of the Dawn Treader.* New York: Macmillan, 1952.

Lindskoog, Kathryn Ann. *The Lion of Judah in Never-Never Land.* Grand Rapids: Eerdmans, 1973.

Manlove, Colin. *The Chronicles of Narnia: The Patterning of a Fantastic World.* New York: Twayne, 1993.

Milton, John. *Complete Poems and Major Prose.* Ed. Merritt Y. Hughes. Indianapolis: Bobbs-Merrill, 1957.

Reader's Digest. *Stories behind Everyday Things.* Pleasantville, N.Y.: Reader's Digest, 1980.

Sayer, George. *Jack.* 2nd ed. Wheaton, Ill.: Crossway, 1994.

Schakel, Peter J. *Reading with the Heart.* Grand Rapids: Eerdmans, 1979.

Schofield, Stephen, ed. *In Search of C. S. Lewis.* South Plainfield, N.J.: Bridge, 1983.

Shakespeare, William. *The Riverside Shakespeare.* Ed. G. Blakemore Evans. Boston: Houghton Mifflin, 1974.

Shelley, Percy. "Ozymandias." Abrams Vol. 2, 535.

Sheridan, Richard Brinsley. *The Rivals.* Ed. Elizabeth Duthie. New York: Norton, 1979.

Spenser, Edmund. *Edmund Spenser's Poetry.* Ed. Hugh Maclean. New York: Norton, 1982.

Sturluson, Snorri. *The Prose Edda.* Trans. Jean I. Young. Cambridge: Bowes and Bowes, 1954.

Tolkien, J. R. R. *The Return of the King.* New York: Ballantine, 1965.

Vaughan, Henry. "Son-days." DiCesare, 157.

Wilson, A. N. *C. S. Lewis: A Biography.* New York: Fawcett, 1990.

Wycherley, William. "The Way of the World." *Plays of the Restoration and Eighteenth Century.* Ed. Dougald MacMillan and Howard Mumford Jones. New York: Holt, Rinehart, and Winston, 1931.